| | | DATE DUE | | |
|---|---|---|---|---|
| | | | | |
| | | | | |
| | | | | |
| | | | | |
| | | | | |
| | | | | |
| | | | | |
| | | | | |
| | | | | |
| | | | | |
| | | | | |

OF

RS

N

## OTHER TITLES IN THE GREENHAVEN PRESS LITERARY COMPANION SERIES:

THE GREENHAVEN PRESS
*Literary Companion*
TO BRITISH LITERATURE

# A PORTRAIT OF THE ARTIST AS A YOUNG MAN

Clarice Swisher, *Book Editor*

David L. Bender, *Publisher*
Bruno Leone, *Executive Editor*
Bonnie Szumski, *Series Editor*

Greenhaven Press, Inc., San Diego, CA

Every effort has been made to trace the owners of copyrighted material. The articles in this volume may have been edited for content, length, and/or reading level. The titles have been changed to enhance the editorial purpose. Those interested in locating the original source will find the complete citation on the first page of each article.

Library of Congress Cataloging-in-Publication Data

Readings on A portrait of the artist as a young man / Clarice Swisher, book editor.
    p.    cm. — (The Greenhaven Press literary companion to British literature)
    Includes bibliographical references and index.
    ISBN 0-7377-0360-1 (lib. bdg. : alk. paper). —
ISBN 0-7377-0359-8 (pbk. : alk. paper)
    1. Joyce, James, 1882–1941. Portrait of the artist as a young man. 2. Dublin (Ireland)—In literature. 3. Young men in literature. I. Title: Portrait of the artist as a young man. II. Swisher, Clarice, 1933–   . III. Series.
PR6019.O9 P64765   2000
823'.912—dc21                                        99-055868
                                                           CIP

Cover photo: Archive Photos

Copyright ©2000 by Greenhaven Press, Inc.
PO Box 289009
San Diego, CA 92198-9009
Printed in the U.S.A.

> **_Welcome, O life! I go to encounter for the millionth time the reality of experience and to forge in the smithy of my soul the uncreated conscience of my race. Old father, old artificer, stand me now and ever in good stead._**
>
> —James Joyce, *A Portrait of the Artist as a Young Man*

# Contents

## Chapter 1: Earlier Models for *A Portrait*

## Chapter 2: Themes, Symbols, and Structure in *A Portrait*

ardly through time, they do follow an underlying order marked by the seasons of the year and the feast days of the church. In places the episodes follow the rhythm of the tides.

## Chapter 3: The Characterization of Stephen Dedalus

## Chapter 4: Joyce's Literary Techniques and Devices in *A Portrait*

Then Stephen recasts the bird image into a positive symbol of his own destiny, but because of its original negative associations, it retains uneasy and fearful undertones.

# FOREWORD

> *"'Tis the good reader that*
> *makes the good book."*
>
> Ralph Waldo Emerson

The story's bare facts are simple: The captain, an old and scarred seafarer, walks with a peg leg made of whale ivory. He relentlessly drives his crew to hunt the world's oceans for the great white whale that crippled him. After a long search, the ship encounters the whale and a fierce battle ensues. Finally the captain drives his harpoon into the whale, but the harpoon line catches the captain about the neck and drags him to his death.

A simple story, a straightforward plot—yet, since the 1851 publication of Herman Melville's *Moby-Dick*, readers and critics have found many meanings in the struggle between Captain Ahab and the whale. To some, the novel is a cautionary tale that depicts how Ahab's obsession with revenge leads to his insanity and death. Others believe that the whale represents the unknowable secrets of the universe and that Ahab is a tragic hero who dares to challenge fate by attempting to discover this knowledge. Perhaps Melville intended Ahab as a criticism of Americans' tendency to become involved in well-intentioned but irrational causes. Or did Melville model Ahab after himself, letting his fictional character express his anger at what he perceived as a cruel and distant god?

Although literary critics disagree over the meaning of *Moby-Dick*, readers do not need to choose one particular interpretation in order to gain an understanding of Melville's novel. Instead, by examining various analyses, they can gain numerous insights into the issues that lie under the surface of the basic plot. Studying the writings of literary critics can also aid readers in making their own assessments of *Moby-Dick* and other literary works and in developing analytical thinking skills.

The Greenhaven Literary Companion Series was created with these goals in mind. Designed for young adults, this unique anthology series provides an engaging and comprehensive introduction to literary analysis and criticism. The essays included in the Literary Companion Series are chosen for their accessibility to a young adult audience and are expertly edited in consideration of both the reading and comprehension levels of this audience. In addition, each essay is introduced by a concise summation that presents the contributing writer's main themes and insights. Every anthology in the Literary Companion Series contains a varied selection of critical essays that cover a wide time span and express diverse views. Wherever possible, primary sources are represented through excerpts from authors' notebooks, letters, and journals and through contemporary criticism.

Each title in the Literary Companion Series pays careful consideration to the historical context of the particular author or literary work. In-depth biographies and detailed chronologies reveal important aspects of authors' lives and emphasize the historical events and social milieu that influenced their writings. To facilitate further research, every anthology includes primary and secondary source bibliographies of articles and/or books selected for their suitability for young adults. These engaging features make the Greenhaven Literary Companion Series ideal for introducing students to literary analysis in the classroom or as a library resource for young adults researching the world's great authors and literature.

Exceptional in its focus on young adults, the Greenhaven Literary Companion Series strives to present literary criticism in a compelling and accessible format. Every title in the series is intended to spark readers' interest in leading American and world authors, to help them broaden their understanding of literature, and to encourage them to formulate their own analyses of the literary works that they read. It is the editors' hope that young adult readers will find these anthologies to be true companions in their study of literature.

# INTRODUCTION

R.B. Kershner, editor of the 1993 edition of *A Portrait*, calls James Joyce "arguably the most influential modern writer in the Western world." Because Joyce's new literary techniques for conveying emotion and experience have influenced twentieth-century writers from realists to postmodernists, to read any serious modern novel is indirectly to read Joyce. He began experimenting with new techniques when he wrote the stories for *Dubliners;* he introduced the techniques in *A Portrait;* and he refined them in *Ulysses* and *Finnegans Wake.*

In *A Portrait of the Artist as a Young Man* Joyce presents the thoughts, impressions, feelings, and experiences of Stephen Dedalus from childhood to young manhood as he becomes an artist. No traditional narrator is in command of relating the storyline. Instead, the reader must decipher the dual voices of a narrator and of Stephen at various ages, both of which are expressed in stream-of-consciousness, internal monologues, and epiphanies that together confound a linear plot progression.

This Greenhaven Literary Companion is designed to help the reader understand and appreciate Joyce's work. The story of Stephen leaps forward by days and years, but not randomly; structurally, it follows the seasons of the calendar year and the festivals of the church year. Motifs, symbols, and images shift and interconnect to engage and stimulate the reader's imagination, emotions, and sense of humor. *A Portrait* has been praised by critics since its publication, is widely taught in high schools and colleges, and remains a popular choice of young people for their own reading pleasure.

Studying Joyce for his place in literary history is important, and particularly significant is the study of *A Portrait*, for here the reader encounters a pioneer in modernism. This volume addresses the important elements of Joyce's language, structure, and style.

# JAMES JOYCE: A BIOGRAPHY

Nearly all of James Joyce's works are autobiographical. "What can a man know," exclaimed James to his brother Stanislaus, "but what passes inside his own head?"[1] Later Joyce reflected on the special difficulties facing the autobiographical novelist "when your work and life make one, when they are interwoven in the same."[2] By turning his life into fiction as he lived it, Joyce developed a detachment from what was happening to him. He knew he could reorder his life and change his perspective on events for the purposes of the book; at the same time, however, he depended on actual events for material. To make ordinary, daily happenings fit his artistic plan, he gave them as extreme a form as possible. While his three novels, *A Portrait of the Artist as a Young Man, Ulysses,* and *Finnegans Wake,* are all set in his native Dublin, Joyce lived in four cities—Dublin, Trieste, Zurich, and Paris. What happened to him in Dublin during his first twenty years is the subject of *A Portrait.*

## FAMILY ORIGINS

James Joyce was born on February 2, 1882, in Rathgar, a Dublin suburb, where he lived until 1887, when his family moved to the fashionable neighborhood of Bray near the sea. His parents, John and May Joyce, had ten children—four boys, and six girls—as well as three infants who did not survive birth. James Augusta was the oldest living child, followed by Margaret, Stanislaus, Charles, George, Eileen, Mary, Eva, Florence, and Mabel, who was born in November 1893. John Joyce worked in the office of collector of rates for Dublin, a well-paid political appointment promised for life. To meet the needs of his growing family and his own spending habits, he added to his income by taking out eleven mortgages on family property in Cork until he lost all of it.

John Joyce, who was born in Cork in 1849, proudly claimed to be a descendant of the noble Galway clan. John's father died when John was seventeen; he subsequently entered Queen's College, Cork, to study medicine. A talented singer and athlete, John neglected his studies and failed his second and third year, and when he got involved in Fenian activities aimed at overthrowing British rule in Ireland in 1874 or 1875, his mother intervened and took him to Dublin. There on May 5, 1880, in the Church of Three Patrons, he married Mary Jane (May) Murray, whom he had met in the Catholic church choir.

Mary Jane Murray, a fair, attractive woman born in May 1859, was ten years younger than her husband. The couple married against the wishes of May's father, who worried about John's drinking and his jealousy, and John's mother, who thought May beneath their class. May's father worked for a distillery as a salesman of wines and spirits. Her maternal relatives, the Flynns, provided her with a musical background; from age five to fifteen she attended the Misses Flynn School, where she studied voice, piano, dancing, and manners. Music played an important part in the personal and public life of the Joyce family. When James was six, he sang with his parents in an amateur concert, and singing around the piano was a common family activity.

James earned the nickname "Sunny Jim" because he was a pleasant, well-behaved little boy. He received preschool education from a governess, Mrs. Dante Hearn Conway, a good Catholic woman who lived with the Joyces after the man she had married ran off. Joyce said she was more superstitious than religious; she scared the children with stories about the end of the world and made them pray when it thundered. From Mrs. Conway, Joyce learned reading, writing, geography, and math until it was time for him to start kindergarten at Miss Raynor's, where he attended with Eileen Vance, his Protestant friend who lived across the street. Dante disapproved of Jim's association with Eileen for fear she might give this good little Catholic boy some "wrong" thoughts.

## JOYCE ENTERS ELEMENTARY SCHOOL

In the fall of 1888, John Joyce enrolled his oldest son in the prestigious Clongowes Wood College, located forty miles from their home in Bray. Run by the Jesuits, Clongowes stated that its aims were to curb the bully and develop the independent personality, goals implicit in the classroom and on the athletic field. Biographer Herbert Gorman explains:

The "independent personality" was also the objective of the recreations at Clongowes. The broad playing fields, green-grassed and beautifully kept, that flank one side of the castle and the new buildings were and are continually alive with the darting figures of boys during the periods of play. Running with them, urging them on, may be seen the black-gowned figures of the prefects.[3]

Joyce was popular, a good athlete, and a good student who was also active in plays and concerts. Several of Joyce's Clongowes experiences make their way into *Portrait:* Joyce was pushed by fellow students into the ditch, or cesspool; Father James Daly (the basis for the fictional Father Dolan) did punish him for breaking his glasses; and he did protest the punishment as unfair to the rector, Father Conmee.

Likewise, the famous Christmas quarrel in *Portrait* did occur in Joyce's life. The incident erupted over the controversial Irish politician Charles Parnell, member of the House of Commons who favored independence, or "home rule" for Ireland. John Joyce had supported Parnell and had discussed him many times with John Kelly of Tralee, a visitor who often stayed in the Joyce household (Mr. Casey in *Portrait*). When, on December 24, 1889, news broke of Parnell's ten-year affair with the wife of W.H. O'Shea, an M.P. from Galway, John Joyce and John Kelly stuck by the man who remained a symbol of independence. Mrs. Conway, however, argued that Parnell's immoral behavior made him an unworthy leader. The ensuing Christmas quarrel was loud enough that the Vances across the street heard it. Mrs. Conway left four days later and did not return to the Joyces.

In June 1891 John Joyce withdrew James from Clongowes when he lost his job in the collector general's office, left with a small pension amounting to a third of his salary. Forty-two years old and entrenched in the habit of drinking in bars with his friends, he blamed his misfortunes on imaginary enemies and turned on his family because the money needed to support them curtailed his drinking. Denying reality, he saw himself as a rich man who "suffered reverses," yet all along his family slid quietly into poverty. In 1892 he moved his family to Blackrock, where James studied on his own for a year while the other children attended a convent school. The next move in 1893 took the family into the city of Dublin to the last house in a respectable location, where for a year all of the children attended schools run by the Christian Brothers, a Catholic monastic order. Joyce never referred to this two-year break from his Jesuit education in any of his books because he felt he was getting less of an education and was ashamed. He believed that the Christian Brothers were the "drones" in Catholic education and the Jesuits the "gentlemen."[4] Coincidentally, in 1893 John Joyce met Father John Conmee, the former rector of Clonglowes, who remembered James's ability. Currently at the Jesuit day school, Belvedere College, he offered to arrange for James and later his brother Stanislaus to attended Belvedere for free.

## JOYCE ENTERS HIGH SCHOOL

James entered Belvedere at age eleven on April 6, 1893, as a student of Grammar III. The architecturally beautiful Belvedere House was built in 1775 for George Rochfort, second earl of Belvedere, and sold to the Jesuits in 1841. They purchased the adjoining residence and added a gymnasium on one side and a chapel, classrooms, and laboratories to complete the quadrangle. Gorman says, "The result was one of the most comfortable and best-equipped Jesuit town schools in Ireland."[5] At Belvedere James respected his English teacher George Stanislaus Dempsey (Mr. Tate in *Portrait*), who encouraged James's love of the English language and his early literary and artistic inclinations. The incident in *Portrait* in which Mr. Tate accuses Stephen of heresy in one of his themes happened in Mr. Dempsey's class. Like Stephen, Joyce was later harassed by fellow students on the street because he disagreed with their opinion of the best poet.

By the time Joyce entered Belvedere, he had a reputation with his family and his teachers for being studious and intelligent. In his book *My Brother's Keeper*, Joyce's brother Stanislaus tells how Joyce's mother occupied him with lessons from his books and lengthy examinations, hoping to keep him busy while she finished her housework; in half the expected time, he was back asking for more. This habit continued, Stanislaus recalled, "until much later, when we were both at Belvedere and he was in the junior grade."[6] In his diary, Stanislaus describes his brother's thirst for knowledge: "Jim has a wolflike intellect, neither massive nor very strong, but lean and ravenous, tearing the heart out of his subject."[7] Besides English, Joyce excelled in Latin, French, and Italian, but was less successful in chemistry. Every spring he prepared diligently for the yearly national examinations and from 1894 to 1897 took top prizes for which he received twenty or thirty pounds. With his prize money he treated his family to plays and restaurants, renewing his father's fantasy that he was a man of social standing. By age fifteen, when Joyce was spending time reading books he had borrowed from the lending library, he studied less for the examinations and in 1898 won only the prize for English composition.

Joyce's home life starkly contrasted with his success at school. In February 1894 Joyce accompanied his father to Cork to sell off the last of the property to pay mortgages, a trip that closely resembled the one Stephen takes with his father in *Portrait.* With the last of the property gone, the family endured a series of moves starting in 1894, each time to humbler accommodations. Besides his pension of eleven pounds per month, John Joyce had a small income from odd jobs as a calligrapher or advertisement canvasser for the *Freeman's Journal,* but the total provided neither adequate food nor decent clothing for the family. The atmosphere at home was tense. When John came home drunk, he often physically abused one of the boys (though never James, his favorite) and frightened the girls with verbal abuse. Shortly after the death of the infant Freddie, John attacked his wife. Stanislaus Joyce describes the scene:

> In a drunken fit he ran at her and seized her by the throat, roaring, 'Now, by God, is the time to finish it'. The children who were in the room ran screaming in between them, but my brother [James], with more presence of mind sprang promptly on his back and overbalanced him so that they tumbled to the floor. My mother snatched up the two youngest children and escaped with my elder sister to our neighbour's house. I remember that a police sergeant called a few days after this pretty scene, and had a long talk in the parlour with my father and mother. . . . Nothing else came of it except that there was no further actual violence, though we lived amid continual threats of it.[8]

Such scenes wearied Joyce, who gradually learned to avoid the unpleasantness when he could and to develop an attitude of indifference when he could not. James, however, recalled a few fond memories mixed in with the squalor. For example, on Sundays John took James and Stanislaus on long walks during which James engaged in conversations with his father, but the conversations ignored Stanislaus, who grew to dislike his father as much as his father disliked him. Stephen's relationship with his father in *Portrait* more closely resembles Stanislaus's relationship with John Joyce than it resembles James's.

Other incidents from Joyce's Belvedere years appear in the novel in altered form. Joyce had his first sexual experience at fourteen with a young maidservant who worked for the Joyces, and shortly after another experience with a prostitute. Suspicious, the rector of Belvedere questioned Stanislaus, who told him the truth, and then reported to Mrs. Joyce that her son was inclined to evil ways. Biographer Richard Ellmann says, "James merely laughed and called him [Stanislaus] a fathead, while Mrs. Joyce blamed the servant and discharged her."[9] Shortly after his introduction to sex, Joyce attended the Belvedere retreat, which began on November 30, 1896, with Father James A. Cullen delivering the customary sermons honoring the feast day of St. Francis Xavier, the patron saint of Belvedere College. Joyce listened to the admonitions and pleadings of the Jesuit father about the power of religion over perturbed minds, and his own scruples and moral beliefs reacted against his recent sexual behavior; Ellmann says, "He saw himself as a beast, eating like a beast, lusting like a beast, dying like a beast, and dreamed of a pure love for a virgin heart."[10] After the retreat Joyce made a confession at the Church Street chapel, where a monk listened sympathetically, and for a time Joyce voluntarily followed strict Catholic discipline. When Joyce was sixteen, the Jesuits recommended that he become a priest, but he already felt that the priesthood was an imprisonment, and he already had committed his life to art. On one of his walks Joyce saw a girl standing in the water with her skirts wrapped around her, an image that came to him just as he was looking for a symbol for his art.

Joyce graduated in 1898 as the highest-ranking senior student. As Ellmann reports, "Belvedere College had done well for Joyce, by giving him excellent training in English and three foreign languages."[11] He liked the Jesuits because they taught him how to order material to make it easy to analyze, but Joyce liked detail, as he later told his friend Frank Budgen, and ordering came easily; "I have a grocer's assistant's mind,"[12] he said. Ellmann continues, "More than that, [Belvedere] had supplied him with a decorous backdrop for his turbulent uprisings and downgoings, a standard against which he would set his own standard. . . . The image of what he must leave behind was almost complete."[13]

## JOYCE ENTERS THE UNIVERSITY

In the fall of 1898, at age sixteen and a half, Joyce, "fairly tall, steely-blue-eyed, and with quite definite ideas about life and letters,"[14] entered University College in Dublin. The college, founded in 1853 by John Henry Newman as the Catholic University, was taken over by the Jesuits in 1883. It occupied grand houses facing St. Stephen's Green, a grassy square with fountains and flowers. Across from St. Stephen's Green stands the National Library of Dublin, referred to as the library of the University College, whose own library was poor. The college faculty was adequate, but not challenging enough for Joyce in English. Fortunately Joyce found in his Italian instructor a sympathetic, liberal teacher who provided him, his only student, with a grounding in Dante and other Italian writers.

At the university Joyce became an independent scholar, reading on his own and developing his ideas with friends. Mostly he read literature from Europe, habitually reading every work by a selected author before going on to another. Joyce found important college friends, listeners, and critics with whom he sharpened his ideas; many of them became characters in *Portrait.* George Clancy—Davin—was an Irish-language enthusiast from the small town of Limerick. Francis Skeffington—McCann—was considered a brilliant student, but odd because he was "a teetotaller, mainly a vegetarian, a feminist, and a pacifist."[15] Another gifted friend, Thomas Kettle, does not appear in *Portrait,* but it was he who discussed Irish politics and Thomas Aquinas with Joyce. Sharing a musical interest with Joyce, Vincent Cosgrave—Lynch—took Joyce to hear the Palestrina choir and copied Gregorian chants and other music for him. Joyce shared his interest in poetry with Oliver St. John Gogarty, who won the poetry prize at Trinity College, the Protestant college in Dublin. Joyce's closest friend was John Francis Byrne—Cranly—who shared poems with Joyce and defended Joyce's poems against the dean of students' criticism. Stanislaus Joyce says: "He used to listen to my brother's theories, and then, so to speak, ring them on the counter and try them between his strong, even teeth."[16] With these friends Joyce formed his opinions on art and the family and his objections to the church and the state, and discovered that perhaps he needed to leave Ireland.

Joyce had begun writing as a young boy. When he was a senior at Belvedere, he compiled his poems into notebooks entitled *Moods* and *Shine and Dark*, wrote a play, *A Brilliant Career*, and composed a series of epiphanies. In his first year at University College, as a member of the Literary and Historical Society, he heard papers and criticized the presenters' ideas. On January 20, 1900, he presented his own paper, "The Drama and Life," using a discussion of Norwegian playwright Henrik Ibsen to illustrate his theory that art has no purpose other than "the imperative inward necessity for the imagination to re-create from life its own ordered synthesis."[17] On the day Joyce read his paper, he received a reply to his letter to W.L. Courtney, editor of *Fortnightly Review*, to which he had offered to submit an article on Ibsen. Courtney's reply asked Joyce instead to send a review of Ibsen's *When We Dead Awake;* Joyce immediately wrote the requested review, which was published in the April 1, 1900, issue. His fellow students were dumbfounded, especially that Joyce was paid twelve guineas for the article. On April 23 Joyce received a message from Ibsen sent through his translator, William Archer. It read:

> I think it will interest you to know that in a letter I had from Henrik Ibsen a day or two ago he says "I have read or rather spelt out, a review by Mr. James Joyce in the *Fortnightly Review* which is very benevolent ('velvillig') and for which I should greatly like to thank the author if only I had sufficient knowledge of the language."

Five days later Joyce replied to Archer: "I wish to thank you for your kindness in writing to me. I am a young Irishman, eighteen years old, and the words of Ibsen I shall keep in my heart all my life."[18]

In the fall of 1901, Joyce submitted a third important essay, "The Day of the Rabblement," to the school magazine, the *St. Stephen's*. It began by quoting an Italian writer who said that no one "can be a lover of the true or the good unless he abhors the multitude" and went on to attack the Irish Literary Theatre "of prostituting the highest form of art (the drama) to the rabblement of the most belated race in Europe."[19] When the article was censored, Joyce had it printed at his own expense and distributed it. By the end of his university days, Joyce knew in his mind what the artist must do, though he had yet to develop his style.

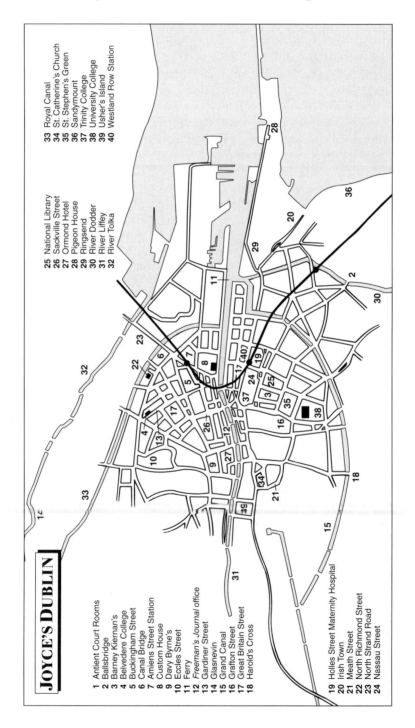

**JOYCE'S DUBLIN**

1 Antient Court Rooms
2 Ballsbridge
3 Barney Kiernan's
4 Belvedere College
5 Buckingham Street
6 Canal Bridge
7 Amiens Street Station
8 Custom House
9 Davy Byrne's
10 Eccles Street
11 Ferry
12 *Freeman's Journal* office
13 Gardiner Street
14 Glasnevin
15 Grand Canal
16 Grafton Street
17 Great Britain Street
18 Harold's Cross
19 Holles Street Maternity Hospital
20 Irish Town
21 Meath Street
22 North Richmond Street
23 North Strand Road
24 Nassau Street
25 National Library
26 Sackville Street
27 Ormond Hotel
28 Pigeon House
29 Ringsend
30 River Dodder
31 River Liffey
32 River Tolka
33 Royal Canal
34 St. Catherine's Church
35 St. Stephen's Green
36 Sandymount
37 Trinity College
38 University College
39 Usher's Island
40 Westland Row Station

## JOYCE LEAVES DUBLIN

After Joyce was graduated from University College in June 1902, having passed but not excelled, he spent the next two years trying to find his niche in Irish society. He enrolled in medical school, but he lacked money and disliked the discipline required for biology, chemistry, and physics courses. He met Irish writers—George Russell, William Butler Yeats, Padraic Colum, and Lady Gregory—who encouraged him, but he felt confined by their ideas. At the beginning of December he went to Paris, fusing this 1902 departure with the 1904 departure in *Portrait*. There he tried medical school, but the sciences were too demanding in French; he tried giving English lessons and found but one pupil. After a trip home for Christmas, he was back in Paris in January 1903, earning a little from reviews, borrowing money and sponging meals, and writing poems and epiphanies. His father called him home in April 1903 because his mother was ill with cancer, and he stayed for over a year. May Joyce's death on August 13, 1903, at forty-four years of age, was an emotional blow for Joyce at a time when he had neither money nor direction. During the chaos following his mother's death, he started drinking. Nevertheless, he managed to write a piece, a blend of essay and story, entitled "A Portrait of the Artist" and submitted it to a new intellectual journal named *Dana*, but it was rejected with this editor's comment, "I can't print what I can't understand."[20]

Then on June 10 Joyce met Nora Barnacle on Nassau Street. Having recently arrived in Dublin from Galway City, she worked as a maid at Finn's Hotel. They met again on June 16. Nora had only a grammar school education, no understanding of literature, and no inclination for inner reflection, but she had wit and a spirited personality. Joyce fell in love with Nora. He became calmer and shed the loneliness he had felt since his mother's death. Ellmann says: "To set *Ulysses* on this date was Joyce's most eloquent if indirect tribute to Nora, a recognition of the determining effect upon his life of his attachment to her. . . . June 16 was the sacred day that divided Stephen Dedalus, the insurgent youth, from Leopold Bloom, the complaisant husband."[21] While Joyce felt better, his situation continued to be dismal. The squalor at home was unbearable, and he had no money. At the suggestion of writer George Russell, he submitted stories to *Irish*

*Homestead* and sold "The Sisters" in August and "Eveline" and "After the Race" before the year's end, three stories that marked the beginning of *Dubliners*. He also sold five poems, but the total payment was insufficient to live on.

Joyce decided to leave Dublin again, asked Nora to leave with him, and she agreed, after which Joyce arranged for a job teaching English at the Berlitz School in Zurich. To obtain travel money, Joyce asked his friends and fellow writers for loans and gifts, and they complied because they thought he had promise as a writer and respected his need to see Ireland from a distance. When he had enough money to get to Paris, he and Nora left Dublin on October 9, 1904; in Paris he again sought gifts and loans to take the couple to Zurich. There he learned he had no job in the Berlitz School, but the administrator felt sorry for him and found one in Pola, south of Trieste, in northeast Italy. This pattern of going ahead without money and somehow borrowing or begging enough to get by dominated Joyce's operation for the next ten years. Even when Joyce was earning a substantial income from his books, he spent so lavishly that he was frequently broke and had to resort to his begging and borrowing ways.

## A MEAGER LIVING IN TRIESTE

Nora and Joyce lived in Pola only one year before they moved to Trieste, where a job had opened in the Berlitz School. Joyce taught English lessons with a flair that made him popular with pupils; when the company lost money, however, Joyce was laid off, and he went to Rome to work as a bank teller, a job he hated and held only a short time. While in Rome Joyce realized how much Dublin had influenced him, and he formulated the acceptance of this realization into a theme for "The Dead." Returning to Trieste, he again found ways to earn a meager living, teaching at the Berlitz School, taking private pupils for English lessons, and writing articles on Ireland for the newspaper the *Piccalo*. He delivered a lecture series in Italian on Ireland, and took exams to qualify him for teaching at the Italian school Sculo Superiore di Commercio Revoltella in the mornings. Though none of his work earned an adequate income, the couple managed to get by.

Joyce and Nora had two children while they lived in Trieste. A son, George (Georgio), was born on July 27, 1905, and named after Joyce's brother George, who had died at fourteen from peritonitis following typhoid fever. On July 26, 1907, a daughter, Lucia Anne, was born in the pauper's hospital. Gorman reports Joyce's reaction to a growing family:

> With three to provide for out of a precarious livelihood he was to be seen more often than ever dashing from house to house in Trieste to give his English lessons and the day was to come when he mockingly remarked that he had taught everybody in town the English language and would have to move on to another city.[22]

Shortly after the birth of Georgio, Joyce missed his family and Dublin ties and longed for conversations with his brother. Late in 1905 Joyce persuaded Stanislaus to come to Trieste to live and procured a job for him at the Berlitz School. Stanislaus served as a sounding board for Joyce's ideas and a critic of his stories, but just as important was his help in organizing Joyce's life and supplementing his income. Joyce also kept his ties with Aunt Josephine, who sent newspapers, magazines, and books on Ireland, and researched the details of some Dublin place Joyce needed for a story. On one of his visits to Ireland, Joyce brought his sister Eileen back with him; she stayed and married a Czech man in Trieste. Ellmann says of Joyce and Ireland, "He could not exist without close ties, no matter in what part of Europe he resided; and if he came to terms with absence, it was by bringing Ireland with him, in his memories, and in the persons of his wife, his brother, and his sister."[23]

In 1903 Stanislaus wrote in his diary that his brother thrived on the excitement of events, creating a nervous tension at home and frequently throwing the family life into chaos. The presence of three or four adults and two children living in a small flat made order difficult, and Joyce seldom stayed in one flat for long. Unskilled in managing money, he repeatedly depended on his brother's generosity; with his own paycheck he took his family to restaurants or spent it drinking in bars. When it was nearly time for Nora to deliver her second child, she had to take in washing when Joyce was hospitalized with rheumatic fever. Both Stanislaus and Nora became disgusted. In 1907 Nora threatened to write home to Galway that she was living with a man who could not support her; when he started for the café one night, she cried, "Yes, go now and get drunk. That's all you're good for."[24] His brother's and wife's anger were enough to make Joyce swear off drinking in early 1908.

During the decade in Trieste, Joyce made three visits to Dublin. On the first, in July 1909, he took Georgio, whom the Joyce family was delighted to see. Joyce wandered around Dublin seeing it again, meeting old friends, and collecting images in his mind for his writing. One conversation with his college friend Cosgrave, who intimated that he had dated Nora and been sexually involved with her, devastated Joyce. He wrote impulsively to Nora on August 7, 1909, "I have been a fool. I thought that all the time you gave yourself only to me and you were dividing your body between me and another. . . . Perhaps they laugh when they see me parading 'my' son in the streets. . . . O, Nora, is there any hope yet of my happiness? Or is my life to be broken?" After Joyce's friend Byrne told him that Cosgrave had been lying, Joyce wrote again to Nora on August 19: "Don't read over those horrible letters I wrote. . . . My darling, forgive me. I love you and that is why I was so maddened only to think of you and that common dishonourable wretch. Nora darling, I apologise to you humbly."[25] Joyce made this experience part of Leopold Bloom's day in *Ulysses*. After visiting Nora's family in Galway City, Joyce returned to Trieste on passage paid for by Stanislaus. A month later Joyce returned to Dublin to set up a theater funded by two Italian businessmen, a venture that soon failed. In 1912 all four members of the Joyce family visited relatives in Dublin and Galway.

### WRITING AND TRYING TO PUBLISH IN TRIESTE

During his ten years in Trieste, Joyce worked hard on his writing but was unable to publish any of it. He submitted new stories to *Irish Homestead*, but he could sell none. He developed the rejected piece, "A Portrait of the Artist," into a novel, entitled *Stephen Hero*, a story that had grown to five hundred pages by the end of 1905. A collection of poems from his student days he compiled into a book he called *Chamber Music* even though he did not like it, calling it "a young man's book."[26] He had a contract with Elkin Mathews for *Chamber Music*, but it was delayed. He sent *Dubliners* to publisher Grant Richards, who objected to scenes and language in some of the stories; after delays Joyce tried another publisher with no better success. He finished "The Dead," and added it to *Dubliners*. He decided to rewrite *Stephen Hero* and call the book *A Portrait of the Artist as a Young Man*, which would portray the gestation of a soul developed in images. In November 1907 he conceived his plan for *Ulysses.* While he was working on *Portrait,* he wrote the play *Exiles* and the first two episodes of *Ulysses.*

After nearly ten years of frustration seeking publishers for his work, Joyce received two letters late in 1913. The first, from Grant Richards, said he wanted to see *Dubliners* again. The second was from Ezra Pound, a wealthy American friend of Yeats who collected stories for two American magazines and was connected with the publication the *Egoist* in London, and who wanted to see Joyce's work. In January Joyce sent Pound *Dubliners* and the first chapter of *Portrait.* Pound immediately made arrangements with Dora Marsden, editor of the *Egoist,* to publish *Portrait* in serial form beginning on Joyce's birthday, February 2, 1914. Grant Richards published *Dubliners* on June 15, 1914, without receiving any objections to language or scenes. Ellmann notes two good reviews of the stories:

> Ezra Pound in the *Egoist* (July 15, 1914) insisted that they marked a return of style into English prose and the introduction of a new subject-matter into Irish literature. Gerald Gould, in the *New Statesman* (June 27, 1914), saw in the stories evidence of the emergence of a man of genius.[27]

Joyce finished *Portrait* and sent the last pages to Pound in August 1915.

## WORLD WAR I AND A MOVE TO ZURICH, SWITZERLAND

In the meantime, World War I had broken out on July 28, 1914, when Austria declared war on Serbia, but Joyce, though near the area of fighting, continued to work in Trieste until Italy entered the war in May 1915. Because Stanislaus had associated himself with an outspoken anticlerical group, he was arrested in January 1915 and sent to an Austrian detention center for the duration of the war. Joyce, told to evacuate, left his furniture and books and moved his family to Zurich, Switzerland, in June 1915 and stayed there until the war was over.

Zurich offered Joyce the kind of excitement that exhilarated him, and he soon adjusted to the new city. Gorman describes Zurich:

> A flood of foreigners driven in by the warring nations jabbered in a dozen tongues in the streets. Refugees, people expelled from enemy territory, war profiteers, spies, deserters, interned soldiers, personalities of pacific or artistic temperament who desired to avoid a world gone mad, shady fellows

with shifty eyes seeking questionable adventures, all these
sought the haven of neutrality that was Switzerland and con-
centred [sic] on Zurich.[28]

In Zurich Joyce used his days to work on *Ulysses* and to give
English-language lessons, which introduced him to friends
and brought needed income. At night Joyce continued his
habit of socializing in cafés and restaurants. At one of his fa-
vorites, the Restaurant zum Weisses Kreuz, a group of men
calling themselves the Club des Etrangers met weekly,
among them Paul Phokas, a Greek speaker who taught his
language to Joyce, and Paul Ruggiero, who spoke Italian
with Joyce and became his English pupil. His closest and
most important friend was Frank Budgen, who enjoyed the
same kind of night life that Joyce liked. According to biographer Sydney Bolt, "But Budgen also served at least as a partial substitute for Stanislaus, as the confidant with whom he
could discuss his writing as it progressed. Budgen wrote an
account of these discussions—*James Joyce and the Writing of
"Ulysses"*—valuable for its insight into the novel."[29] With his
gregarious personality Joyce was soon well known in Zurich
and had a wide circle of friends.

News of Joyce's financial troubles spread among his admirers, who felt he should spend his time writing rather than
teaching. Pound and Yeats arranged for the prime minister of
England to award Joyce a Civil List grant in August 1916 and
obtained a small grant from the Society of Authors. Joyce also
received a monthly remittance from Nora's uncle and from an
American millionairess. Harriet Weaver, who edited the *Egoist*, admired the truthfulness in Joyce's work and sent him
monthly remittances for the rest of his life. Opera soprano
Charlotte Sauermann arranged with Mrs. Harold McCormick,
daughter of John D. Rockefeller Sr., to provide Joyce with a
thousand francs each month. Gorman says: "It seemed like
manna from heaven to Joyce for it meant that he could relieve
himself from some part of his arduous teaching and devote
this freed time to the formidable problems of *Ulysses*."[30]

## JOYCE'S SOCIAL AND FAMILY LIFE

Though Joyce finally had the financial means to live an orderly life, it was not his nature to do so and his nervous energy continued to create a hubbub. He involved himself in
the organization and management of a semiprofessional acting company, the English Players, with plans for productions

in Zurich and nearby Swiss towns. The first play, Wilde's *The Importance of Being Earnest,* went smoothly until an amateur actor named Carr objected to his salary. Insults ensued and small sums of money were disputed and Joyce, in the manner of the schoolboy at Clongowes, took the matter to authorities and insisted on justice. After quarrels and litigation with British officials, he won a few francs and gave the offensive officials parts as foul-mouthed brutes in *Ulysses.* Moreover, Joyce's family had to endure the turmoil he created. Besides uprooting the family by moving three times during the four years in Zurich, he was away from home managing the players and attending performances. At one point Georgio accused his parents of shutting their children up like pigs in a sty.

In spite of Joyce's frenetic activities, Nora and the children got on well enough in Zurich. Georgio and Lucia, who knew no German, were put back two years in school when they came to Zurich, but they learned the language and advanced in their grades. Georgio made friends, participated in sports, and studied music, but Lucia suffered from the frequent moves. Nora, steadfastly devoted to her husband, graciously accepted his friends, but not his excessive drinking, which he had resumed. Disgusted one day, she scared him by saying she had torn up his manuscript, a threat that sobered Joyce on the spot. Though he shared none of his intellectual or writing life with Nora, he depended on her and was loyal to her except for a few brief interests in other women. He was attracted to Marthe Fleischmann, a young woman he noticed on a Zurich street, because she resembled the girl he had seen wading by the shore on one of his boyhood walks in Dublin, the bird-girl in *Portrait.* For three months the two exchanged letters and met, but both knew nothing serious would come of the relationship. He still described himself as he did in Trieste: "I, who am a real monogamist and have never loved but one in my life."[51]

Joyce worried most in Zurich about his worsening eye problems, which had begun in Trieste and became acute in February 1917. One day on the street he was overcome by severe pain from an attack of glaucoma, a painful eye disease caused by abnormally high fluid pressure in the eye, a condition that if left untreated damages the retina and eventually leads to blindness. After four weeks' recovery in a darkened room, he had another attack, but recovered enough to write again by June. In August, following a third severe attack, his ophthalmologist, Professor Ernst Sidler, operated on his right eye. The operation was successful, but slightly reduced his vision. A year later, in May 1918, Joyce suffered from iritis, the inflammation of the irises in both eyes, a serious but less painful condition that did not prevent him from continuing his activities with the players or his writing. These recurring illnesses affected his peace of mind, and he worried that perhaps he might go blind.

## WRITING AND WORKING WITH PUBLISHERS

In Zurich Joyce again dealt with publishers. In July 1916 the American publisher B.W. Huebsch agreed to publish *Portrait* in New York, and on December 29 released its first edition anywhere; in February 1917 Harriet Weaver brought out an English edition. Yeats, Lady Gregory, and T.S. Eliot liked it, H.G. Wells praised it in a review for the *Nation,* and other thoughtful and complimentary reviews followed. The play *Exiles,* which Joyce had finished in Trieste, was plagued by delays. Publisher Grant Richards held it for several months before publishing it in May 1918. It received good reviews, and Joyce wanted to see it produced on stage in England, but again there were delays. Finally translator Hannah von Mettal completed a German translation, which was produced in Munich in August 1919 but poorly received by German audiences.

Joyce's greatest energy went into writing *Ulysses,* the book he had begun planning in 1907. He had completed the first two of eighteen planned episodes and he wrote eleven more in Zurich. Pound arranged with American publishers Margaret Anderson and Jane Heap to publish *Ulysses* in serial form in *Little Review* beginning in March 1918. Now Joyce had deadlines requiring him to send Pound completed episodes on a regular schedule. In London Harriet Weaver wanted to publish *Ulysses* in serial form in the *Egoist,* but until early 1919 she had trouble finding a typesetter who did not object to the language and content.

*Ulysses* portrays a day in the life of Leopold Bloom in his travels around Dublin; the episodes allude to the travels of Ulysses in the *Odyssey.* Frank Budgen describes Joyce's intense involvement:

> Joyce's preoccupation with his book was never ending. He was always looking and listening for the necessary fact or word; and he was a great believer in his luck. What he

needed would come to him. That which he collected would prove useful in its time and place. And as, in a sense, the theme of 'Ulysses' is the whole of life, there was no end to the variety of material that went into its building.[32]

Joyce built the episodes on people he met and experiences he had. When he began an episode, he wrote down a series of phrases; as the episode took shape in his mind, he coded the phrases with colored pencils to indicate where they should go. He said that writing a novel was like composing music, incorporating chords and motifs into the work; for example, he might repeat a motif, such as "kidney," with different meanings and uses in different chapters.

When World War I ended, Joyce and his family moved back to Trieste and reunited with Stanislaus and Eileen. Though saddened by the loss of Irish friends who were killed in the war, Joyce was otherwise unaffected by and indifferent to it. Asked for comment, he said, "Oh yes, I was told that there was a war going on in Europe."[33] After the excitement of Zurich, his old language-teaching job in Trieste bored him, and life in this quiet city seemed dull. Ezra Pound suggested that Joyce move to Paris, and Joyce agreed.

## PARIS AND THE PUBLICATION OF *ULYSSES*

Joyce and his family arrived in Paris on June 23, 1920. Ezra Pound, already living there, had done his work as Joyce's advance agent. He suited Joyce in new clothes and "took Joyce from salon to salon, exhibited him with the pride of an expert showman . . . [to] all the French writers of the moment."[34] Before long Joyce was frequenting the cafés with his new Parisian friends and living the same frenzied life he had lived in Zurich. The American wife of a Japanese painter said quietly to Nora, "You are a martyr to a man of genius."[35] Nora, who had grown tired of the upheaval and drinking, took the children to Ireland and threatened not to return; shortly after their arrival, however, fighting broke out in Ireland, and they were forced to return. Nora had grown equally irritated at the way Joyce unabashedly used people to do things for him. She told him, "If God Almighty came down to earth, you'd have a job for him."[36]

As in Zurich Joyce was again busy overseeing publications. Pound found a French translator for *Portrait,* which was published in 1924, and another publisher came to Joyce to arrange for a German translation. Some of the serialized episodes of *Ulysses* had raised censorship issues in America over frank language and sexual content and as Joyce finished the episodes, he worried if censorship problems would prohibit its publication in book form. Sylvia Beach, who had opened a bookshop in Paris, Shakespeare and Company, offered to help Joyce publish *Ulysses* in France with backing of the *Egoist*. When Joyce finally received the page proofs for corrections, he expanded the book by a third, which meant further publication delays. Joyce, who wanted a birthday edition, got his wish; on February 2, 1922, Sylvia Beach received two advance copies, one for Joyce and one to display in her shop, to which a steady stream of people came all day to see it. *Ulysses* was translated into German and French, but an English edition did not come out until 1936, when the censorship ban was lifted. In 1933 a judge lifted the ban in America, and Random House published it in January 1934. Joyce, who also wanted *Exiles* produced successfully, was satisfied when a 1925 New York production ran for forty-one nights; a London company produced it in 1926, but the play never became a hit.

Completing *Ulysses* was a major accomplishment; the book had consumed Joyce's energies for sixteen years and taken seven years to write. He said he had spent twenty thousand hours writing it, an average of more than eight hours every day for seven years. When he finished the Circe episode in December 1920, he had written it eight or nine times. Joyce believed that in *Ulysses* he had "joined the best possible words (English) to the best possible subject matter (Irish)."[37] He always wrote about Dublin because he knew he could get into the heart of Dublin, and he believed if he could get into the heart of Dublin, he could get into the heart of all cities in the world. "In the particular is contained the universal,"[38] he said.

The publication of *Ulysses* caused a sensation among writers and Parisians. T.S. Eliot said that Joyce had ended nineteenth-century style and started something new. Virginia Woolf thought it a "book by a self taught working man." Ernest Hemingway wrote, "Joyce has a most goddamn wonderful book." Irish playwright and novelist George Moore said, "*Ulysses* is hopeless; it is absurd to imagine that any good end can be served by trying to record every single thought and sensation of any human being. That's not art, it's like trying to copy the London Directory." French dramatist André Gide called it "a sham masterpiece." Yeats's first thought was "A mad book!" but he later said, "I have made a terrible mistake. It is a work perhaps of genius. I now perceive its coherence."[39] When Joyce went to restaurants in Paris, crowds gathered to look at the man who had written this strange book, and he had to change his habits to avoid them.

## FAMILY ISSUES

The decade following the publication of *Ulysses* included significant family events, some happy, some sad. Joyce was happy that his brother Stanislaus, who was forty-two, planned to marry Nelly Lichensteiger, but right after that good news, he learned that his sister Eileen's husband had committed suicide while Eileen was in Ireland. Nora, who had always been healthy, became ill; in February 1929 surgery required a long hospital stay; Joyce, refusing to be separated from her, had a bed put in the room and stayed there with her. After a short banking career, Joyce's son Georgio turned to a full-time singing career; his teacher thought he had the talent to become a concert singer, but Georgio lacked the discipline to succeed, partly because he had met Helen Fleischman. He and Helen married in December 1930; in 1932 the couple had a son whom they named Steven James Joyce in honor of his grandfather. Thinking now about inheritance and about passing on the family name, Joyce thought he and Nora should be married. They attempted a quiet ceremony in England in 1931, but Joyce's celebrity drew reporters and their pictures appeared in the paper. It amused Joyce to marry the woman who had been his wife for twenty-seven years. Before the year was out Joyce received word that his father was terminally ill. Though John Joyce had begged his son to visit him once more, Joyce could not overcome his sense of exile and return to Ireland; when his father died on December 29, Joyce felt guilty as well as sad.

Joyce's most unnerving family problem was Lucia, who began manifesting strange behavior in 1930. Joyce involved her in lessons in piano, voice, dancing, and drawing, but she grew progressively more disoriented and was unable to continue. She became increasingly hostile toward Nora and one day threw a chair at her. She was diagnosed with schizophrenia when she was twenty-five. Because Joyce wanted to keep Lucia out of institutions, he tried several arrangements with private nurses, but her increasing irrationality finally forced her institutionalization. A letter from her in October 1934 indicated that her madness had progressed. Making arrangements for Lucia and worrying about her interrupted his work on his novel-in-progress, *Finnegans Wake.*

### JOYCE WRITES AND PUBLISHES *FINNEGANS WAKE*

In 1923, shortly after the publication of *Ulysses,* Joyce gradually formed ideas for a sequel to *Ulysses,* a book he was to work on for sixteen years. As *Ulysses* is a "day" book, *Finnegans Wake* is a "night" book, requiring a special language. Joyce explained:

> I have put the language to sleep. . . . In writing of the night, I really could not, I felt I could not, use words in their ordinary connections. Used that way they do not express how things are in the night, in the different stages—conscious, then semiconscious, then unconscious. I found that it could not be done with words in their ordinary relations and connections. When morning comes of course everything will be clear again. . . . I'll give them back their English language. I'm not destroying it for good.[40]

By the end of 1923 Joyce had sketched out most of the eight chapters, composing the first of four parts. In them he introduced pub owner Earwicker, his wife Anna Livia Plurabelle, their three children, and other characters. Only Nora knew the title, and she had sworn not to reveal it to anyone.

Joyce did not want this book serialized, but in April 1924 he sent a fragment to appear in the *Literary Supplement* entitled *Work in Progress,* the title he used until the book was published in 1939 with the title *Finnegans Wake.* When he showed segments to his friends, their reaction was negative. Harriet Weaver spoke of it as "wallowing in verbiage."[41] Joyce's brother did not like it, and other friends were critical. When Joyce became so depressed he could not sleep, Nora asked, "Why don't you write sensible books that people can understand?"[42] Finally he decided his best answer to his critics was to keep writing. When he finished it, he had again produced something quite original. As Ellmann notes:

> In his earlier books Joyce forced modern literature to accept new styles, new subject matter, new kinds of plot and characterization. In his last book he forced it to accept a new area of being and a new language. What is ultimately most impressive is the sureness with which, in the midst of such tech-

nical accomplishments, he achieved his special mixture of attachment and detachment, of gaiety and lugubriousness.[43]

*Ulysses* had paved the way with censors, and because few could actually understand *Finnegans Wake*, there were fewer publication problems, but Joyce was nonetheless impatient with delays because he could see that war was about to break out and worried that people would be too preoccupied to read his book. On May 4, 1939, *Finnegans Wake* was published simultaneously in London and New York. Hundreds of reviews appeared, but, according to Joyce, only about one in ten had even a glimmer of insight.

## JOYCE'S FINAL DAYS

Joyce had spent uneasy years leading up to the publication of his last book. He was nervous about its reception and occupied with the care of Lucia; his daughter-in-law had had a mental breakdown and was hospitalized; and he was still suffering from eye disease. While in Paris, he had had ten eye operations and had lost some of his sight. When Yeats invited him to join the Academy of Irish Letters, he refused, too depressed ever to return to Ireland. Following the outbreak of World War II in 1939, Paris fell to the Germans in June 1940, and Joyce made arrangements to go back to Zurich, arriving there on December 17. He spent Christmas with his family and friends.

At a restaurant party on January 9, 1941, he was overtaken with stomach pain and taken to the hospital. There X rays showed that Joyce had a perforated duodenal ulcer, and he underwent surgery immediately on Saturday, January 11. The operation seemed to be successful, but his condition was unstable, and he fell into a coma on Sunday; at the urging of the doctor, Nora and Georgio went home. Joyce woke from the coma during the night and asked for his wife and son, who were summoned, but before they arrived, Joyce died, at 2:15 A.M. on January 13, 1941. He was buried after a simple ceremony in a hilltop Zurich cemetery. Kenneth Grose writes:

> His best epitaph is that of his long-suffering wife, who had never read his books; when asked about her acquaintance with the great literary figures who had come into her life, she replied, 'Sure, if you've been married to the greatest writer in the world, you don't remember all the little fellows.'[44]

## NOTES

1. Quoted in Kenneth Grose, *James Joyce.* Totowa, NJ: Rowman and Littlefield, 1975, p. 9.

2. Quoted in Richard Ellmann, *James Joyce.* New and revised edition. Oxford: Oxford University Press, 1982, p. 149.

3. Herbert Gorman, *James Joyce.* New York: Rinehart, 1939, p. 31.

4. Ellmann, *James Joyce,* p. 35.

5. Gorman, *James Joyce,* p. 40.

6. Stanislaus Joyce, *My Brother's Keeper: James Joyce's Early Years.* Ed. Richard Ellmann. New York: Viking, 1958, p. 45.

7. George Harris Healey, ed., *The Dublin Diary of Stanislaus Joyce.* Ithaca, NY: Cornell University Press, 1962, p. 15.

8. Joyce, *My Brother's Keeper,* p. 56.

9. Ellmann, *James Joyce,* p. 48.

10. Ellmann, *James Joyce,* p. 49.

11. Ellmann, *James Joyce,* p. 56.

12. Quoted in Ellmann, *James Joyce,* p. 28.

13. Ellmann, *James Joyce,* p. 56.

14. Gorman, *James Joyce,* p. 56.

15. Joyce, *My Brother's Keeper,* p. 110.

16. Joyce, *My Brother's Keeper,* p. 172.

17. Joyce, *My Brother's Keeper,* p. 128.

18. Both letters quoted in Ellmann, *James Joyce,* p. 74.

19. Quoted in Joyce, *My Brother's Keeper,* pp. 144–45.

20. Quoted in Ellmann, *James Joyce,* p. 147.

21. Ellmann, *James Joyce,* p. 156.

22. Gorman, *James Joyce,* p. 145.

23. Ellmann, *James Joyce,* p. 292.

24. Quoted in Ellmann, *James Joyce,* p. 268.

25. Richard Ellmann, ed., *Selected Letters of James Joyce.* New York: Viking, 1975, pp. 159–60.

26. Quoted in Ellmann, *James Joyce,* p. 232.

27. Ellmann, *James Joyce,* p. 353.

28. Gorman, *James Joyce,* p. 231.

29. Sydney Bolt, *A Preface to James Joyce.* London: Longman, 1981, p. 20.

30. Gorman, *James Joyce,* pp. 237–38.

31. Quoted in Bolt, *A Preface,* p. 21.

32. Quoted in Gorman, *James Joyce,* pp. 238–39.

33. Quoted in Ellmann, *James Joyce,* p. 472.

34. Gorman, *James Joyce,* p. 272.
35. Quoted in Ellmann, *James Joyce,* p. 491.
36. Quoted in Ellmann, *James Joyce,* p. 699.
37. Ellmann, *James Joyce,* p. 505.
38. Quoted in Ellmann, *James Joyce,* p. 505.
39. Quoted in Ellmann, *James Joyce,* pp. 528–30.
40. Quoted in Ellmann, *James Joyce,* p. 546.
41. Quoted in Ellmann, *James Joyce,* p. 594.
42. Quoted in Ellmann, *James Joyce,* p. 591.
43. Ellmann, *James Joyce,* p. 717.
44. Grose, *James Joyce,* p. 17.

## WORKS CONSULTED

Sydney Bolt, *A Preface to James Joyce.* London: Longman, 1981.

Richard Ellmann, *James Joyce.* New and revised edition. Oxford: Oxford University Press, 1982.

——, ed., *Selected Letters of James Joyce.* New York: Viking, 1975.

Herbert Gorman, *James Joyce.* New York: Rinehart, 1948.

Kenneth Grose, *James Joyce.* Totowa, NJ: Rowman and Littlefield, 1975.

George Harris Healey, ed., *The Dublin Diary of Stanislaus Joyce.* Ithaca, NY: Cornell University Press, 1962.

Stanislaus Joyce, *My Brother's Keeper: James Joyce's Early Years.* Ed. Richard Ellmann. New York: Viking, 1958.

# Characters and Plot

## Main Characters

*Stephen Dedalus:* a boy of Dublin, Ireland, portrayed from early childhood to his days at the university.

*Simon Dedalus:* Stephen's father, a proud man whose efforts to support his family end in social and financial failure.

*Mrs. Dedalus:* Stephen's mother, a full-time mother guiding and supporting her children.

*Maurice Dedalus:* Stephen's brother.

*Uncle Charles:* Stephen's elderly maternal granduncle.

*Dante Riordan:* a widow who has lived for a time in the Dedalus household, perhaps as a governess ("Dante," a corruption of "auntie," is a term of familiarity and affection); a critic of the powerful Protestant politician Charles Stewart Parnell.

*Mr. Casey:* a friend of the Dedalus family and supporter of Parnell.

*Eileen Vance:* Stephen's Protestant friend.

*Students at Clongowes:* Rody Kickham; Nasty Roche; Jack Lawton; Simon Moonan; Fleming; and Wells, who pushes Stephen into a ditch filled with water.

*Brother Michael:* the head of the infirmary at Clongowes when Stephen is sick.

*Father Dolan:* a prefect of studies at Clongowes, the administer of discipline, who punishes Stephen for not reading when his glasses are broken.

*Rev. John Conmee:* the rector at Clongowes, to whom Stephen describes his unjust punishment.

*EC:* the initials of Emma Clery, of whom Stephen is enamored.

*Students at Belvedere:* Wallis; Boland; Nash; and Vincent Heron, Stephen's chief rival.

*Father Arnell:* the priest who delivers the sermons at the Belvedere retreat.

*Students at university:* Cranly, Davin, McCann, Moynihan, Temple, and Lynch.

## PLOT

*A Portrait of the Artist as a Young Man* chronicles the life of Stephen Dedalus, the son of a Catholic family in Dublin, Ireland, from early childhood through his university days. The novel records Stephen's sensations, impressions, daydreams, thoughts, experiences, emotions, and epiphanies in unconnected nonchronological episodes, leaving the reader to make the connections among them and tease out their meaning. These episodes are unified, not around events, but around the theme of the development of a soul.

Chapter 1 opens from the perspective of a young child hearing his father tell a fairy tale, dancing as his mother plays the piano, and being taken to the playground. When old enough for school, Stephen is enrolled in Clongowes, a boarding school, where he interacts with other boys, attends prayers, and notices new words and sentences. Wells, one of the students, chides Stephen about kissing his mother and pushes him into a ditch filled with dirty water. He awakens the next morning sick and is sent to the infirmary, where Brother Michael cares for him and helps him write a note to his parents, asking them to come to get him. Waiting in the infirmary, he visualizes his own death and funeral.

At home for the Christmas holidays, Stephen is allowed for the first time to eat Christmas dinner with the adults instead of in the nursery. During dinner a political argument breaks out. Stephen's father Simon Dedalus, and Mr. Casey, who support the disgraced Irish nationalist Charles Stewart Parnell, disagree with Dante Riordan, who condemns him. Mr. Casey pounds his fist, Dante leaves the table, and Mr. Casey and Stephen's father weep for the dead Parnell. The holiday dinner breaks up leaving Stephen confused and wondering whom to trust.

After the holidays Stephen returns to Clongowes and resumes his confused observations of the behavior of other boys. When he is pushed down and his glasses are broken, he thinks of his friend Eileen, and her white hands and gold hair. During a writing lesson in Mr. Hartford's class, the prefect, Mr. Dolan arrives and punishes Fleming for writing a bad theme by hitting his extended palms with a pandybat. Because Stephen was not working—he had been told not to work because his glasses were broken—the prefect administers the same punishment to him. Humiliated and angered, Stephen complains about his unfair treatment to the rector, Father Conmee, who listens and says he will talk to Mr. Dolan. Stephen returns to his schoolmates, who gather round with questions and praise his nerve and success.

In chapter 2 the Dedalus family moves twice, and Stephen changes schools. The family moves first to Blackrock, a south Dublin suburb, and shortly after to Dublin proper, both moves to lower-cost housing made necessary by Simon Dedalus's financial problems. Stephen knows he will not return to Clongowes, but he will attend Belvedere College, a Jesuit grammar school for boys, on a scholarship Father Conmee has helped him obtain.

During this summer in the Blackrock suburb, Stephen makes friends and explores the neighborhood. He and Aubrey Mills drive with the milkman and form a gang of adventurers. From his Dublin city home, he roams the streets surrounding his house and walks to the docks, where he observes stevedores loading and unloading ships. He visits relatives with his mother and attends a children's party. In all of his activities, however, he feels different from others. At Belvedere he acts in a play and within two years has achieved the status of second in his class. His chief rival is Vincent Heron, who with Wallis bullies Stephen and humiliates him. He defends an essay which Mr. Tate condemns as heresy, and he acts in another play. A street encounter with Heron, Boland, and Nash begins amicably with a discussion of poets and ends when the three boys beat Stephen with a cane and cabbage stumps. He has become confused by conflicting messages he receives from various sources: He is by his upbringing urged to be a gentleman and a good Catholic; his school urges him to be strong, manly, and patriotic; and his peers pressure him to be decent, never to snitch, and to use his influence to get time off school. None of these messages rings true for Stephen.

Stephen travels by train with his father to Cork to sell off property for money to pay debts. Affecting a proud attitude, Simon shows his son the school he attended and the haunts where he and his friends enjoyed their youth. They end the day in a bar where Simon drinks to past memories. As the chapter closes Stephen wins an essay contest and uses the prize money to treat his family to elegant gifts, trying to relieve their current squalor. Dismayed when his plan fails, he wanders the streets and visits a prostitute.

Chapter 3 opens as Stephen circles home through the brothel district, aware that his visit to the prostitute is a sin, aware that he could be sent to hell any minute; he feels guilty, but not sorry enough to pray. The school rector announces the required retreat honoring Father Xavier, the patron of Belvedere. During the retreat the boys are to withdraw to examine their consciences, reflect on the mysteries of religion, and contemplate the meaning of their existence. Father Arnell delivers sermons on death, judgment, hell, and heaven, all of which the reader hears as Stephen perceives them. After a vivid description of death and an explanation of personal and final judgment, Stephen is pensive. After the sermon on sin and the physical description of hell as a dark, crowded place, one boy declares that "He put us all into a blue funk," but Stephen feels guilty and vows to confess. After the sermon on the spiritual torment of hell, Stephen returns to his room, where he prays on his knees and envisions his own hell. Although he could have accepted the invitation to confess and repent in the school chapel, Stephen instead seeks a confessional in an unfamiliar church away from the school, where his "sins trickled from his lips, one by one." Receiving absolution, he feels happy and proud of his decision, and vows to do penance at home and at school.

As chapter 4 opens, Stephen begins his program of devotion and discipline to atone for his sins. He says rosaries for faith, hope, and love and prays for seven gifts of the Holy Ghost to drive out the seven deadly sins. He brings each of his senses under strict discipline: He makes a rule to walk with downcast eyes and shun every encounter with the eyes of women. He makes no effort to control the sounds of his changing voice, he neither sings nor whistles, and he never flees from irritating sounds that jangle his nerves. Not usually bothered by bad smells, he vows to subject himself whenever possible to the one fishy smell that revolts him. He practices all of the fasts of the church to the letter and tries not to notice and enjoy good food at regular meals. His most inventive rules involve his sense of touch; he vows never to change his position in bed, never to respond to an itch or pain, to leave parts of his neck and face wet so that the air might sting them, and to walk with his arms held stiffly at his side.

Despite his efforts, Stephen is flooded with temptations and feels guilty for being angered by small irritations. He tires of his rigorous routine of self-denial and concludes that he will always be a sinner. His behavior, however, has caught the attention of the director, who summons him and invites him to join the Jesuit order. Upon reflection, Stephen realizes he is repelled by a priest's loss of freedom and visualizes a priest's face filled with "suffocated anger." He decides he will not choose the priesthood, that he will seek engagement with the world and others; "disorder, the misrule and confusion of his father's house" has won over his soul. He watches a line of priests cross a bridge, ordered by legend, color, and tradition; Stephen chooses to order his life by words. He sees an image of the Greek myth of Daedalus and Icarus and vows to create, as the "great artificer whose name he bore, a living thing, new and soaring and beautiful." In a vision birds call to his soul, and an image of a woman standing in the water poised as a bird symbolizes his possibilities. For Stephen this experience is an epiphany, a realization that he wants a secular life, that his allegiance is to nature, and that he will "create life out of life."

In chapter 5, Stephen is a student in the university, a position his father has procured for him. Having chosen his life goal, Stephen attends classes sporadically; when his parents nag and manipulate him to leave the house for classes, he wanders through a Dublin slum before he arrives for physics, his third class of the day. Much of chapter 5 takes place on the library porch, where students gather for intellectual talk and college wit. On long walks, Stephen has several conversations with fellow students. In one he rejects Irish nationalism and talks of the nets of nationality, language, and religion that he will try to fly past. In a conversation with Lynch he works out his theory of aesthetics. To his confidant Cranly, he explains his break with his mother over his unwillingness to profess his Catholic faith publicly. Birds circle the library steps and Stephen watches, recognizing them as symbols of departure or loneliness; Ireland has become claustrophobic. The novel ends with his plans to leave for Paris. He keeps a diary through March and April recording his activities, thoughts, and dreams. In the next-to-last entry, his mother packs his new secondhand clothes and prays for her son. Stephen welcomes his new life: "I go to encounter for the millionth time the reality of experience and to forge in the smithy of my soul the uncreated conscience of my race." In his last entry he calls on his old father Daedalus of the ancient Greek myth to stand him in good stead.

# CHAPTER 1

# Earlier Models for *A Portrait*

# Dante Is a Model for Joyce

Joseph Campbell

Joseph Campbell argues that James Joyce modeled *A Portrait* on "La Vita Nuova," a poem written between 1290 and 1294 by the Italian poet Dante, author of the *Divine Comedy*. Campbell draws several parallels: In the center of both works a crisis occurs, out of which the Holy Spirit speaks through a woman. Both authors comment on the poetic structure of their works, and both go forth to pioneer new forms of literature. Joseph Campbell, who taught at Sarah Lawrence College for almost forty years, is widely considered the world's foremost authority on mythology. He is the author of *The Hero with a Thousand Faces*, the four-volume *The Masks of God*, *The Power of Myth* with Bill Moyers, and many other books.

Joyce's model for this book [*A Portrait of the Artist*] was Dante's[1] *La Vita Nuova, The New Life*. What is the New Life? The New Life is the awakening in a person's life of a spiritual (as opposed to an economic, political, or social) trajectory or aim or dynamic. This birth of the spiritual life in a human animal is what is called the virgin birth. We share with the animals certain zeals: we hang on to life to beget future lives, we fight to gain and to win. But another life goal can be awakened.

When Dante first saw Beatrice, she was nine years old and so was he. She was wearing a scarlet dress. In the Middle Ages, scarlet was the color of the Christ. Dante said, "Beatrice is a nine because her root is in the Trinity." She was transparent to transcendence; and he looked at her, not with the eye of lust—that is, not with desire—but with

---

1. Italian poet Dante Alighieri; in early life he fell in love with a girl whom he celebrates under the name of Beatrice in "La Vita Nuova" and the *Divina Commedia*.

Excerpts edited from *Mythic Worlds, Modern Words: On the Art of James Joyce*, by Joseph Campbell, edited by Edmund L. Epstein (New York: HarperCollins, 1993). Copyright ©1993 by the Joseph Campbell Foundation. Reprinted with permission from the Joseph Campbell Foundation (www.jcf.org). Quotations in Mr. Campbell's text from *A Portrait of the Artist as a Young Man* are copyrighted ©1916 by B.W. Huebsch, ©1944 by Nora Joyce, ©1964 by the Estate of James Joyce, and used by permission of Viking Penguin, a division of Penguin Putnam, Inc.

awe at her beauty as a manifestation of the radiance of God's love for the world. By hanging onto that awe and remaining in that meditation, which was the meditation of his entire life, he was carried to the throne of God. That was Dante's meditation.

In *Portrait* there are several women who play decisive roles in Stephen's awakening spiritual life, as the female aspect did in Dante's. At first, when Stephen is a little boy, there are little girls; but he is a very precocious boy, and as he gets older he begins to follow what is called "the left-hand path."

> He burned to appease the fierce longings of his heart before which everything else was idle and alien. He cared little that he was in mortal sin, that his life had grown to be a tissue of subterfuge and falsehood. Beside the savage desire within him to realise the enormities which he brooded on nothing was sacred.

In Dublin in those days there was a large brothel section, and there Stephen, while still a boy in prep school, has found, you might say, the female aspect in its dark side.

## A CRISIS IN THE CENTER OF THE BOOK

In the very middle of the *Vita Nuova*, there is a radical shift from the earthly to the transcendent sphere: Beatrice dies, and since Dante no longer has the delight of her physical presence, his meditation is translated to the invisible. And right in the middle of every one of Joyce's books is a similar crisis where the perspective shifts. You can almost find the crisis in one of his books just by opening it to the last page, writing down the page number, dividing it by two, and then turning to that page. This happens in *Ulysses* and in *Finnegans Wake*, and it happens here, at the end of the second section of the *Portrait.*

The New Life is the life of the awakened spiritual, poetic (rather than practical) relationship to the world through the physical realm and the experiences informing it. Here is the emergence of the New Life for Stephen, the crisis in *A Portrait.* If you open the book exactly in the middle, at the start of the third section, you find Stephen, this boy who has got himself into this terrible condition, listening to a hell-sermon by a priest, Father Arnall.

Recall what has brought us to this crisis: Joyce begins with this little boy with his family—you recall, his mother had a nicer smell than his father and so on—and then the boy goes to school, and as he grows, every one of his experiences is translated into its subjective aspect. He internalizes everything, and since he has been trained in Roman Catholic theology, his experiences very soon become linked to that theology. We begin to get the inward sense of Stephen's experiences, and from that understanding, we move into a wonderful expansion of those experiences by way of a mythological interpretation. This dynamic carries right through the whole work.

### THE ANNUAL RETREAT AND THE SERMON ON HELL

Now in Catholic schools, there is usually an annual retreat, where you stop studying and just hear about the spiritual life and think about these things. I can remember that the big number in every retreat was always the sermon on hell. You are sitting there, the priest comes in and describes hell, and then you are a good boy for about the next two weeks. I've heard about six of those sermons in the course of my life. We'd always say, "Here comes the hell-sermon." And some boy would always get sick in the course of it. This is the sermon that Stephen hears:

> —*Hell has enlarged its soul and opened its mouth without any limits*—words taken, my dear little brothers in Christ Jesus, from the book of Isaiah, fifth chapter, fourteenth verse. In the name of the Father and of the Son and of the Holy Ghost. Amen.
>
> The preacher took a chainless watch from a pocket within his soutane and, having considered its dial for a moment in silence, placed it silently before him on the table.
>
> He began to speak in a quiet tone.
>
> —Adam and Eve, my dear boys, were, as you know, our first parents and you will remember that they were created by God in order that the seats in heaven left vacant by the fall of Lucifer and his rebellious angels might be filled again. Lucifer, we are told, was a son of the morning, a radiant and mighty angel; yet he fell: he fell and there fell with him a third part of the host of heaven: he fell and was hurled with his rebellious angels into hell. What his sin was we cannot say. Theologians consider that it was the sin of pride, the sinful thought conceived in an instant: *non serviam: I will not serve.*

*Non serviam: I will not serve.* That is Joyce's motto.

> That instant was his ruin. He offended the majesty of God by the sinful thought of one instant and God cast him out of heaven into hell for ever.

Father Arnall tells the story of the creation of Adam and

Eve, their fall from the garden. Then he describes hell:

> Every sense of the flesh is tortured and every faculty of the soul therewith: the eyes with impenetrable utter darkness, the nose with noisome odours, the ears with yells and howls and execrations, the taste with foul matter, leprous corruption, nameless suffocating filth, the touch with redhot goads and spikes, with cruel tongues of flame. And through the several torments of the senses the immortal soul is tortured eternally in its very essence amid the leagues upon leagues of glowing fires kindled in the abyss by the offended majesty of the Ominipotent God and fanned into everlasting and ever increasing fury by the breath of the anger of the Godhead.
>
> —Consider finally that the torment of this infernal prison is increased by the company of the damned themselves.

Father Arnall describes hell as a place where all of the senses are fiercely tortured. The fire that burns is a dark fire, a horrendous fire that does not consume what it burns. He says: *Place your finger for a moment in the flame of a candle*, and then imagine this pain for eternity over your whole body. Then there is the unbearable stench: *All the filth of the world, all the offal and scum of the world . . . shall run there as to a vast reeking sewer . . .*—that is like the latrine outflow Stephen was shouldered into. The unbreathable air, thick with pestilential odors, suffocates, but you do not die. Your sight is assaulted with horrific visual images. Worst, there is the permanent separation from God, whom you have seen for a moment—the moment of personal judgment when He condemns you to hell, saying: "Go to the fires of eternal death!" And the contrast between the life you have lived— the things you have sought, what you thought was beauty and pleasure—the contrast between that and this momentary experience of what you should have been intending fills you with a dreadful sense of loss.

The aspect of hell is pain. People in hell are people fixed in their temporal interests, people trapped in their ego systems, people for whom the practical world has not become transparent. That is what hell is: a place for people who are fixed forever. And being fixed for eternity is very painful. Every sense is tormented—sound, smell, taste—and a black fire burns but does not consume.

Again, the *Portrait* follows *La Vita Nuova*. When Beatrice dies in the middle of Dante's book, he is transformed by the experience of death and the relationship of the life that he has led to the totality of human potentialities for experience. Similarly, in the middle of the *Portrait*, Stephen is transformed: the hell-fire sermon works. Poor Stephen, who has been a sinner, is suddenly struck with the realization of the degradation of the life he has been leading. His life is amplified into a hell image, the one image the Church has to give that really does something to Stephen, and that image is so fierce, it transforms his character.

Now most kids haven't committed any real sins at all. I mean, they go to confession and say, "Bless me Father, I didn't say my morning prayers three times and I said 'boo' to my mother once." Well, a hell-fire sermon is terrifying even if your only sins are not saying your prayers and disobeying your mother, but Stephen is a boy who has been way, way deep into sin. He is living in what the Church calls "mortal sin"—that is to say, the type of sin that puts a person in hell. And when Father Arnall's sermon is over, Stephen is filled with remorse for the life that he has been leading.

> Could it be that he, Stephen Dedalus, had done those things? His conscience sighed in answer. Yes, he had done them, secretly, filthily, time after time, and, hardened in sinful impenitence, he had dared to wear the mask of holiness before the tabernacle itself while his soul within was a living mass of corruption. How came it that God had not struck him dead?

### STEPHEN'S TRANSFORMATION BEGINS

So Stephen decides to go to confession and repair his life. He goes sneaking around to find another church, where he can confess to a priest whom he does not know. Well, he makes his confession, and the priest, though appalled that this youngster is confessing such sins, gives him his penance. The boy really resolves not to sin this way again. He becomes devoutly religious and—like the schizophrenic who is filled with the impulse to become the king, the hero—he decides he is going to be a saint. He has always wanted to go to the extreme in everything. Now a good way to become a saint or prophet is to become a Jesuit, so he begins to watch the Jesuits. He becomes such a devoted and saintly boy that they begin to think of him as a potential priest. Eventually the director summons Stephen to his office and asks him if he has ever felt like he had a vocation. Then, observing that God calls only a chosen few to the religious life, the priest tells him:

> —To receive that call, Stephen, said the priest, is the greatest honour that the Almighty God can bestow upon a man. No king or emperor on this earth has the power of the priest of

God. No angel or archangel in heaven, no saint, not even the Blessed Virgin herself has the power of a priest of God: the power of the keys, the power to bind and to loose from sin, the power of exorcism, the power to cast out from the creatures of God the evil spirits that have power over them, the power, the authority, to make the great God of Heaven come down upon the altar and take the form of bread and wine. What an awful power, Stephen!

### STEPHEN'S AWAKENING: THE HOLY SPIRIT SPEAKS

But while listening to the director, Stephen thinks about priests who condemn books they haven't read and about how they talk in clichés. The images of the tradition are being communicated by people who have not had equivalent affect[2] experiences; there is a dissociation of image from affect. Stephen, who takes the vow of vocation very seriously to his heart, is aware of this split, of the priests not being what they stand for, so he does not know what path to follow. He wants not just to fall into a job, but to determine what his life is going to be.

Later, at loose ends, he wanders one day on the beach north of Dublin where some of his friends are swimming. Now in *Ulysses*, Stephen declares that he "was hydrophobe," but I think Joyce also was hydrophobic; that is to say, both were afraid of water. The boys swimming call to Stephen—*Stephanos Dedalos! Bous Stephanoumenos! Bous Stephanoumenos!*—addressing him with Greek endings on the words. As they banter and call, Stephen starts to think of himself as lost, not knowing what direction his life is going to take. And it is just after this moment, in this condition, that he encounters the girl in the stream, the experience which opens him to the call of life.

He comes to a little tidal inlet, takes off his sneakers and throws them over his shoulder, and starts wading in the little stream. And then comes this beautiful moment, the awakening:

> He was alone. He was unheeded, happy and near to the wild heart of life. He was alone and young and wilful and wildhearted, alone amid a waste of wild air and brackish waters and the seaharvest of shells and tangle and veiled grey sunlight and gayclad lightclad figures, of children and girls and voices childish and girlish in the air.
>
> A girl stood before him in midstream, alone and still, gaz-

2. feeling or emotion

ing out to sea. She seemed like one whom magic had changed
into the likeness of a strange and beautiful seabird. Her long
slender bare legs were delicate as a crane's and pure save
where an emerald trail of seaweed had fashioned itself as a
sign upon the flesh. Her thighs, fuller and softhued as ivory,
were bared almost to the hips where the white fringes of her
drawers were like featherings of soft white down. Her slate-
blue skirts were kilted boldly about her waist and dovetailed
behind her. Her bosom was as a bird's soft and slight, slight
and soft as the breast of some darkplumaged dove.

It is as though she were a bird, the dove-tailed spirit.

But her long fair hair was girlish: and girlish, and touched
with the wonder of mortal beauty, her face.

She was alone and still, gazing out to sea; and when she
felt his presence and the worship of his eyes her eyes turned
to him in quiet sufferance of his gaze, without shame or wantonness. Long, long she suffered his gaze and then quietly
withdrew her eyes from his and bent them towards the
stream, gently stirring the water with her foot hither and
thither. The first faint noise of gently moving water broke the
silence, low and faint and whispering, faint as the bells of
sleep; hither and thither, hither and thither: and a faint flame
trembled on her cheek.

Stephen does not know who she is, and it does not matter.
Like Dante, he views the girl, not with lust, but in rapture.

—Heavenly God! cried Stephen's soul, in an outburst of profane joy.

The Holy Spirit, in the shape of the dove, has spoken to him
through her. He is in movement now, but not psychologically.

He turned away from her suddenly and set off across the
strand. His cheeks were aflame; his body was aglow; his
limbs were trembling. On and on and on and on he strode, far
out over the sands, singing wildly to the sea, crying to greet
the advent of the life that had cried to him.

She has opened him. She has passed into his soul forever,
as once Beatrice passed into Dante's.

Her image had passed into his soul for ever and no word had
broken the holy silence of his ecstasy. Her eyes had called
him and his soul had leaped at the call. To live, to err, to fall,
to triumph, to recreate life out of life! A wild angel had appeared to him, the angel of mortal youth and beauty, an envoy from the fair courts of life, to throw open before him in
an instant of ecstasy the gates of all the ways of error and
glory. On and on and on and on!

She was, as it were, transparent to transcendence: a call,
not to herself, but to life.

He halted suddenly and heard his heart in the silence. How far had he walked? What hour was it?

The world has dropped off. Time and space are gone in the enchantment of the heart.

There was no human figure near him nor any sound borne to him over the air. But the tide was near the turn and already the day was on the wane. He turned landward and ran towards the shore and, running up the sloping beach, reckless of the sharp shingle, found a sandy nook amid a ring of tufted sandknolls and lay down there that the peace and silence of the evening might still the riot of his blood.

He felt above him the vast indifferent dome and the calm processes of the heavenly bodies; and the earth beneath him, the earth that had borne him, had taken him to her breast.

He closed his eyes in the languor of sleep. His eyelids trembled as if they felt the vast cyclic movement of the earth and her watchers, trembled as if they felt the strange light of some new world. His soul was swooning into some new world, fantastic, dim, uncertain as under sea, traversed by cloudy shapes and beings. A world, a glimmer, or a flower? Glimmering and trembling, trembling and unfolding, a breaking light, an opening flower, it spread in endless succession to itself, breaking in full crimson and unfolding and fading to palest rose, leaf by leaf and wave of light by wave of light, flooding all the heavens with its soft flushes, every flush deeper than the other.

Evening had fallen when he woke and the sand and arid grasses of his bed glowed no longer. He rose slowly and, recalling the rapture of his sleep, sighed at its joy.

He climbed to the crest of the sandhill and gazed about him. Evening had fallen. A rim of the young moon cleft the pale waste of sky like the rim of a silver hoop embedded in grey sand; and the tide was flowing in fast to the land with a low whisper of her waves, islanding a few last figures in distant pools.

Here is an actual, physical, earthly, and spiritual experience, understood in terms of a mythological experience: the impregnation of his soul by the dove, the Holy Spirit, symbolized in this girl, who is the counterpart of Dante's Beatrice. This vision becomes the inspiration of Joyce's life and of all his heroines. The heroine of *Ulysses*, Molly Bloom (who is, so to speak, the gross aspect), is all through that book, although she is never out of bed. When we get to *Finnegans Wake*, the heroine running and flowing throughout that book is Anna Livia Plurabelle, a great female power. This vision of the girl in the stream becomes Stephen's inspiration. It opens him past all of the various conflicts: his family and its situation, his vocation, the clergy's experiences not matching the import of their imagery, and his own confusion. Here is a moment where the imagery suddenly speaks: he sees the girl as a dove, as the Holy Spirit announcing the incarnation. . . .

### JOYCE FOLLOWS DANTE'S FORM

Dante precedes each of the poems in the *Vita Nuova* with a description of the circumstances that brought about its writing, and he follows each of the poems with an analysis of his poetic structure and what he intended to render through that. Joyce does the same here. In the section after his vision on the beach, Stephen describes his esthetic theory to a friend, and then we read about the circumstances surrounding his writing of a little villanelle: a girl had looked at him without shame or wantonness, and without revulsion or desire being invoked; it's an ecstatic moment. So he has translated his esthetic into precise imagery. He is going to be an artist, a celebrator of this image. . . .

We'll pass down to the last dates now.

16 *April*: Away! Away!

The spell of arms and voices: the white arms of roads, their promise of close embraces and the black arms of tall ships that stand against the moon, their tale of distant nations. They are held out to say: We are alone. Come. And the voices say with them: We are your kinsmen. And the air is thick with their company as they call to me, their kinsman, making ready to go, shaking the wings of their exultant and terrible youth.

26 *April*: Mother is putting my new secondhand clothes in order. She prays now, she says, that I may learn in my own life and away from home and friends what the heart is and what it feels. Amen. So be it. Welcome, O life! I go to encounter for the millionth time the reality of experience and to forge in the smithy of my soul the uncreated conscience of my race.

27 *April*: Old father, old artificer, stand me now and ever in good stead.

At the end of the *Vita Nuova*, Dante says, "I now go forth to prepare myself to write of her such a work as has never been written before." And he writes the *Commedia*, enlarging the inspiration that came through Beatrice into a vision of God's world. Stephen (Joyce) does the same. "Old father, old artificer" is Daedalus, the Greek master artist. Emulating him, Stephen flies, so to say, from Dublin; and Joyce undertakes to write *Ulysses*, wherein Stephen will observe:

Fabulous artificer. The hawklike man. You flew. Whereto? Newhaven-Dieppe, steerage passenger. Paris and back. Lapwing. Icarus. *Pater, ait.* Seabedabbled, fallen, weltering. Lapwing you are. Lapwing he.

*A Portrait* ends with:

Dublin 1904
Trieste 1914

Beginning in Dublin in 1904 and finishing in Trieste in 1914, this young man spent ten years writing this little book.

# *A Portrait* as *Bildungsroman*: A Novel of Development

Breon Mitchell

Breon Mitchell provides a brief history of the *bildungsroman*, a coming-of-age novel. He then argues that, though Joyce departs slightly from the form by opening Stephen's story in early childhood rather than in preadolescence, Stephen is a typical *bildungsroman* hero and that Joyce follows the traditional style and structure. Breon Mitchell has taught German and comparative literature at Indiana University. He is the author of *James Joyce and the German Novel: 1922–1933* and essays on Bertolt Brecht, Samuel Beckett, Günter Grass, Franz Kafka, W.H. Auden, and others.

When Joyce first began work on *A Portrait*, the *Bildungsroman* already had a long and established tradition, beginning with the "priceless pages" of [German writer Johann] Goethe's *Wilhelm Meister* [Master]. Thus Joyce could, by implication, play off the development of his young hero against a succession of literary figures from the past. In calling his novel *A Portrait of the Artist as a Young Man*, Joyce simultaneously related it to yet another tradition—the static portraiture of the visual arts. Yet when an artist like Rembrandt painted a self-portrait, he froze the moment at which, looking into a mirror, he paused before applying the brush to the canvas. Joyce was opposed to this frozen mirror of art the notion of organic growth and change in time:

> The features of infancy are not commonly reproduced in the adolescent portrait for, so capricious are we, that we cannot or will not conceive the past in any other than its iron, memorial aspect. Yet the past assuredly implies a fluid succession of presents, the development of an entity of which our actual present is a phase only.

Excerpted from "*A Portrait* and the *Bildungsroman* Tradition," by Breon Mitchell, in *Approaches to Joyce's* Portrait, edited by Thomas F. Staley and Bernard Benstock. Copyright ©1976 by University of Pittsburgh Press. Reprinted by permission of the University of Pittsburgh Press.

This statement, which opens Joyce's 1904 essay "A Portrait of the Artist," points toward the central concept of the *Bildungsroman*, or novel of development.

The *Bildungsroman* first appeared in eighteenth-century Germany and has continued to reappear in almost every national literature of the Western world. Goethe's *Wilhelm Meister* (1795–96) established a model for this new form of the novel and encouraged others to try their hand at it. The influence of *Wilhelm Meister* has been both profound and pervasive. It is safe to say that no major German novel about a young man's development has been written without a backward glance toward Goethe. And to an important degree his influence may be felt in the major novels of development in France, England, and America as well.

## A Definition of the *Bildungsroman*

The notion of the *Bildungsroman* is a simple one: the author treats the life of a young man through the important years of his spiritual development, usually from boyhood through adolescence. He is shown as being formed and changed by interaction with his milieu, and with the world. Experience, as opposed to formal education, is considered central to development. The young man must encounter life, and be formed in that encounter. The *Bildungsroman* is inevitably open-ended: it prepares the hero for maturity and life but does not go on to depict that life; in place of experiencing his destiny the hero is made ready to confront it. There is no guarantee of his success, but there is usually good reason to hope for it. The hero of the *Bildungsroman* also has his characteristic traits. He is normally good-hearted, naïve, and innocent. Often he is completely separated from society by birth or fortune, and the story of his development is the story of his preparation to enter into that society. The *Bildungsroman* thus has as an important concomitant interest the relationship of the individual to society, the values and norms of that society, and the ease or difficulty with which a good man can enter into it.

The basic concerns of the *Bildungsroman* have their effect on the structure and style of the novel as well. The novel is held together as a work of art not by the story (as in a conventional novel) but by our interest in the development of the main character. The action tends to be episodic rather than arranged into a tightly woven plot. The form of the novel is itself "open," rather than, for example, the "closed" circular structure of [James Joyce's] *Finnegans Wake.* Since it is closely concerned with internal development, the *Bildungsroman* also shows a typical texture of narrative techniques suited to such an interest, including inner monologue, narrated monologue, quoted thought, internal analysis, and use of the first person.

In light of even this brief description of the traditional *Bildungsroman*, it is obvious that Joyce's *Portrait of the Artist as a Young Man* is in many ways almost surprisingly conventional, in the literal sense of that term. This is in itself worth pointing out, for Joyce is an author of such inventiveness and originality that points of contact with traditional literary forms are worth holding on to. . . .

## STEPHEN'S DEVELOPMENT FROM EARLY CHILDHOOD

The opening pages of *A Portrait* dip further back into childhood than do most traditional novels of development, and the seemingly random impressions of the small child point to the central themes of the novel to come: art (storytelling), family, politics, incipient love, punishment, and apology, even the foreshadowing of the physical in the initially pleasant unpleasantness of bed-wetting. Almost every major theme is introduced in miniature.

Like Stephen's first step in the aesthetic apprehension of a work of art, the child must begin by separating himself from the rest of reality. Initially the lines of distinction are blurred—he *is* baby tuckoo. On the flyleaf of his geography book at Clongowes he attempts to locate himself physically in space: "He read the flyleaf from the bottom to the top till he came to his own name. That was he: and he read down the page again. What was after the universe? Nothing. But was there anything round the universe to show where it stopped before the nothing place began? . . . It made him very tired to think that way." Gaining a sense of himself is of course one of Stephen's major preoccupations throughout the novel. With his father in Cork, he is later to recite a variant of the same theme in a vain attempt to understand who and where he is: "I am Stephen Dedalus. I am walking beside my father whose name is Simon Dedalus. We are in Cork, in Ireland. Cork is a city." His task is made more difficult by the fact that he is constantly changing. Already by the second chapter of the novel he thinks of his childhood as "dead or lost." He is not yet sixteen years old. Such sensitivity to the very process of growth and change he is experiencing distinguishes Stephen from most of his literary predecessors. He is acutely aware of the rapid disappearance of his past self from moment to moment. Recalling his first premonition of death while in the infirmary at Clongowes he muses: "He had not died but had faded out like a film in the sun. He had been lost or had wandered out of existence for he no longer existed. . . . It was strange to see his small body appear again for a moment." His final decision to reject the life of the church is marked by a passage which might almost serve as an epigraph for the traditional *Bildungsroman*: "He was destined to learn his own wisdom apart from others or to learn the wisdom of others himself wandering among the snares of the world."

### STEPHEN IS A TYPICAL *BILDUNGSROMAN* HERO

Like the typical *Bildungsroman* hero, Stephen begins as a good-hearted and naïve little boy, unable to understand why his older classmates laugh when he says he kisses his mother good night. The correct answer to their questions is beyond him, for he has yet to learn that there is no answer. Later, at Belvedere, the sin of sacrilege and the mysterious sexual offenses hinted at by his schoolmates stand for yet another realm of life beyond his grasp. He feels set apart from the others and dimly perceives that he differs from them in important ways. In this latter respect Stephen resembles the typical *Bildungsroman* hero as well. Traditionally the hero is cut off from society by birth or fortune, and Stephen is certainly dogged throughout the novel by his humiliating sense of grinding poverty and squalor: "The life of his body, illclad, illfed, louseeaten, made him close his eyelids in a sudden spasm of despair." But the feeling of otherness which possesses him goes far beyond economic conditions: "Stephen watched the three glasses being raised from the counter as his father and his two cronies drank to the memory of their past. An abyss of fortune or of temperament sundered him from them. His mind seemed older than theirs: it shone coldly on their strifes and happiness and regrets like a moon upon a younger earth." It is this same sense of spiritual isolation which has left him a spectator since early childhood. The gap that separates him from others cannot be closed by wealth, as he soon learns when his prize money has been quickly spent:

> How foolish his aim had been! He had tried to build a break-water of order and elegance against the sordid tide of life. . . . Useless. . . .
> He saw clearly too his own futile isolation. He had not gone one step nearer the lives he had sought to approach nor bridged the restless shame and rancour that divided him from mother and brother and sister.

It is this unbridgeable spiritual distance which, in the twentieth-century *Bildungsroman*, replaces the more literal exclusion of the hero from society in earlier examples.

The changes Stephen undergoes in the course of the novel, and the choices he is forced to make, arise out of the texture of his everyday life. In the very first chapter he already knows that the tears in his father's eyes must somehow be weighed against Dante's fervent cry "God and religion before everything! . . . God and religion before the world!" Ultimately, he will seek to escape both politics and religion, but for the moment he is a lost and deeply puzzled little boy: "Who was right then?" As he grows older it is the interaction with the world around him which contributes to the formation of his character. His fall into a life of youthful degeneration seems temporarily redeemed by his moral decision to repent and confess. But this too is simply a stage in his spiritual growth, and his rejection of the religious life carries with it a clear commitment to a wider realm of experience:

> The voice of the director urging upon him the proud claims of the church and the mystery and power of the priestly office repeated itself idly in his memory. His soul was not there to hear and greet it and he knew now that the exhortation he had listened to had already fallen into an idle formal tale. He would never swing the thurible before the tabernacle as priest. His destiny was to be elusive of social or religious orders.

For the moment it seems to Stephen as if life, in all its untidiness, has triumphed: "He smiled to think that it was this disorder, the misrule and confusion of his father's house and the stagnation of vegetable life, which was to win the day in his soul." The final choice of a new and higher ordering of life has yet to be made.

When Stephen at last recognizes the true shape of his destiny, he feels that his soul has "arisen from the grave of boyhood, spurning her graveclothes." This was the call of life to his soul not the dull gross voice of the world of duties and despair, not the inhuman voice that had called him to the pale service of the altar." "He would create proudly out of the freedom and power of his soul, as the great artificer whose name he bore, a living thing, new and soaring and beautiful, impalpable, imperishable." The final chapter of *A Portrait* provides the necessary counterweight to these flights of rapture. Poverty and the disorder of life have not miraculously vanished. At the university Stephen must struggle with one last decision—to escape the world he knows, completely.

## *A PORTRAIT* FOLLOWS *BILDUNGSROMAN* STYLE AND STRUCTURE

Not only the content, but also the style and structure of *A Portrait* are in part determined by the particular demands of the *Bildungsroman*. Since interest is focused on Stephen's spiritual progression, the novel tends to be episodic; it is clear that the basic division of the work into five chapters reflects this progression and that each chapter presents us with a distinct stage in Stephen's development. Because that development is far from a smooth path to maturity, it should not surprise us that the narrative line of *A Portrait* has its ups and downs as well. The upbeats come at the end of each of the five sections. Nevertheless, the upswing of emotion and release which occurs in the final pages of each chapter is always balanced by a corresponding deflation in the initial pages of the next.

Thus Stephen's triumph at Clongowes in the first section is followed in the second by his move to Belvedere and his discovery of the true face of the encounter through his father's conversation with the rector. The tears of joy and sexual relief with which the second section closes are transformed into bitter remorse in the third. The power of confession and communion which makes life seem so beautiful and peaceful at the end of the third section soon evaporates in the fourth, leaving only a sensation of spiritual dryness. The profane joy and rapture Stephen experiences on the beach at the close of the fourth section is given its inverse mirror image at the beginning of the fifth in the dark pool of the jar and the squalid life which still surrounds him. The open-ended novel, were this rhythm to continue, would point toward yet another spiritual deflation following his departure from Ireland. And indeed many readers feel a fall is in the offing. Nevertheless, we must concede that the rhythm of *A Portrait* is not the simple movement of a pendulum.

There is a progression toward maturity and self-knowledge, toward the acceptance of both life and error. If we are not convinced that Stephen has, by the end of the novel, achieved a full measure of wisdom, we must at least admit that the path he has traced is close enough to that of the invisible author hovering behind the work to admit the possibility of his ultimate success. Stephen's *Wanderjahre* [travels] still lie before him, but the basic choices have been made, and the important elements of his *Bildung* are all in place.

# CHAPTER 2

# Themes, Symbols, and Structure in *A Portrait*

# The Interrelationship of Theme, Symbolism, and Structure

Elizabeth Drew

*Elizabeth Drew identifies the central theme of* A Portrait of the Artist *as the growing conscience and consciousness of a writer and the ways a gifted "misfit" frees himself from his constraining environment. Drew shows that the symbolism of Stephen Dedalus's name enhances this theme. Elizabeth Drew was a visiting lecturer at Smith College in Massachusetts and a teacher at the Middlebury College Graduate School of English at Breadloaf, Vermont. She is the author of* Discovering Poetry, T.S. Eliot: The Design of His Poetry, *and* Poetry, A Modern Guide to Understanding and Enjoyment.

We must not read the book *A Portrait of the Artist as a Young Man* as straight autobiography. Some critics, indeed, argue that Stephen Dedalus is not James Joyce at all. While that seems most improbable, nevertheless the book is a work of art, not a slice of life, and the materials of the life it creates have been selected, arranged, altered, dramatized and fictionized to support the central theme. They are probably all true to the spirit of Joyce's development, but not necessarily to the facts. The result is an evocation of the growing conscience and consciousness of a dedicated writer and of the warping and uncongenial environment that surrounds him; the story of how a gifted, imaginative and intellectual misfit frees himself from the shackling influence of family, church and society and sets out as an exile to fulfill his vocation.

## STEPHEN FEELS LIKE AN EXILE

Stephen has been a spiritual exile from his social surroundings since early childhood. The description of him in the

Excerpted from *The Novel: A Modern Guide to Fifteen English Masterpieces,* by Elizabeth Drew (New York: W.W. Norton, 1963). Reprinted with permission from the Trustees of Smith College.

football game at Clongowes might be a metaphor for all his participation in the life of his fellows: "He crept about from point to point on the fringe of his line, making little runs now and then." When he is at Belvedere College he champions Byron and Shelley and Ibsen, feels in his schoolmates "a vague general malignant joy" when he is accused of heresy in an essay, and sees himself "proud and sensitive and suspicious, battling against the squalor of his life and the riot of his mind." At the University the students distrust his "intellectual crankery." He feels equally isolated from the church and knows that he could never train for the priesthood: "His destiny was to be elusive of social and religious orders. . . . He was destined to learn his own wisdom apart from others or to learn the wisdom of others himself wandering among the snares of the world." In his own family he is equally apart. He realizes it when he has spent his prize money on trying to restore some order and elegance into the home:

> He saw clearly his own futile isolation. He had not gone one step nearer the lives he had sought to approach. . . . He felt that he was hardly of one blood with them but stood to them rather in the mystical kinship of fosterage, foster child and foster brother.

Again, in his phase of religious devotion, he finds it impossible to combine his pious practices with any human charity toward others: "To merge his life in the common tide of other lives was harder for him than any fasting or prayer."

In spite of "little runs now and then" he remains always on the "fringe" of any corporate life and an exile within his own country. To fulfill himself he must leave Ireland, and he tells his friend Davin why. Davin urges him to be "one of us," that is, a dedicated Irishman. Stephen replies bitterly that Ireland has always rewarded devotion to her cause by betrayal; she is "the old sow who eats her farrow," and he continues:

> When the soul of a man is born in this country there are nets flung at it to hold it back from flight. You talk to me of nationality, language, religion. I shall try to fly by those nets.

## THE SYMBOLISM OF STEPHEN'S NAME

The book is the story of the nets and the escape from them to freedom, and the name of the hero is full of symbolic significance. Stephen is the name of the first Christian martyr. He protested that God's message to the people had been misinterpreted: "which of the prophets have your fathers not persecuted?" But the synagogue said he spoke blasphemy and "they cast him out of the city and stoned him." That Joyce meant this analogy to be drawn is clear when he makes Stephen think of St. Stephen's Green in Dublin as *his* green. Indeed the later treatment of Joyce by Dublin—over the publication of *Dubliners*, and in the banning of his later books—has borne out the parallel. But the surname Dedalus is far more important, since the symbolism surrounding that encloses the whole story from start to finish. It has a double significance for Joyce. The mythical Dedalus was imprisoned in a labyrinth on the island of Crete, and escaped by inventing wings. He is a symbol, therefore, not only of the rebel who breaks out of his prison, but of the inventor who creates the instrument of his escape. He is both man and artist. Etymologically the name means "the cunning one," and the epigraph of the book is a line from [Roman poet] Ovid's *Metamorphoses* which tells of Dedalus making his plans: "And he gave up his mind to obscure arts."

The full force of the analogy reveals itself in the crucial scene of the book, at the end of the fourth chapter. Stephen, having decided flatly against entering the priesthood, in spite of the temptation to power it provides, goes out on the seashore and has a vision of his true vocation. He watches the clouds drifting westward, bound for Europe, and seems to hear "a confused music within him as of memories and names which he was almost conscious of but could not capture even for an instant"—the voices of his tradition. The music recedes and he hears some of his schoolmates calling: "Hello, Stephanos! . . . Here comes The Dedalus!" The boys are bantering him, giving him the title "Stephanos"— "one crowned with wreaths"—and that of the cunning inventor. He recognizes their mockery, but it flatters him:

> Now, as never before, his strange name seemed to him a prophecy. . . . Now, at the name of the fabulous artificer, he seemed to hear the noise of dim waves and to see a winged form flying above the waves and slowly climbing the air. What did it mean? Was it a quaint device opening a page of some medieval book of prophecies and symbols, a hawklike man flying sunward above the sea, a prophecy of the end he had been born to serve and had been following through the mists of childhood and boyhood, a symbol of the artist forging anew in his workshop out of the sluggish matter of the earth a new soaring impalpable imperishable being?
>
> His heart trembled . . . and a wild spirit passed over his limbs as though he were soaring sunward. . . . His soul was

soaring in an air beyond the world and the body he knew was purified in a breath and delivered of incertitude and made radiant. . . . An ecstasy of flight made radiant his eyes and wild his breath and tremulous and wild and radiant his windswept limbs.

The words "soaring" and "radiant" repeat themselves ryhthmically throughout, and this image of flight, of soaring on wings fashioned out of "the sluggish matter of the earth," carrying a body made radiant by spirit, reborn into a new dimension of being—this is the symbol throughout for the identity of the artist. It is echoed in a different key in the scene later on the steps of the library. He watches the wheeling swallows and wonders if they augur good or evil for him, and fear of the unknown seizes him: "a fear of symbols and portents, of the hawklike man whose name he bore . . . of Thoth, the god of writers." Quickly, though, the cry of the birds, the moving patterns of their flight and the words of a poem all melt together in his consciousness. The thought of escape from Ireland and escape into language flow together into a sense of profound release.

### IMAGES OF IMPRISONMENT AND OPPRESSION

In direct opposition to all the images of flight, of the open sky and the open sea of freedom of movement and warm creative zest, "the call of life to his soul," are a whole series of contrasting symbols to suggest the forces of captivity which imprison the young Stephen. Hints of the labyrinth appear in the school corridors, the "maze of narrow and dirty streets," the playground at Clongowes, the racetrack in the park, while later he is to find himself caught in the labyrinth of sin; and his mind "wound itself in and out" as he tries "to grope in the darkness of his own state." In opposition to the images of soaring sunward flight over the sea are many of impeded flight or earthbound heaviness. The greasy football in the game at Clongowes "flew like a heavy bird through the grey light" and the "call of life" is that of the shouting boys and the prefects urging them on. Another vivid scene is where the director of the Jesuits offers Stephen the "secret knowledge and secret power" of the priestly office. Stephen recognizes another "call of life," of which he had often dreamed, but as he imagines himself in the novitiate "his lungs dilated and sank as if he were inhaling a warm moist unsustaining air," and he smelled again the atmosphere of the "sluggish turfcoloured water" in the bath at Clongowes. As a child this produced "a vague fear" and it becomes symbolic of the *stagnation* he feels around him. It is associated with the dark pool of the dripping jar in his sordid home, "scooped out like a boghole." Again, Stephen's mind quickens as he walks with Lynch, discussing the rhythm and vitality of art, but when they come to the canal "a crude grey light, mirrored in the sluggish water, and a smell of wet branches over their heads seemed to war against the course of Stephen's thought." When he looks in at the windows of a smart hotel he wonders how he could arouse the conscience and imagination of the "patricians of Ireland" so that "they might breed a race less ignoble than their own."

> And under the deepened dusk he felt the thoughts and desires of the race to which he belonged flitting like bats across the dark country lanes, under trees by the edges of streams and near the poolmottled bogs.

Five times in the book the soul of Ireland is described as bat-like: blind, verminous, haunting the dark, "flitting" instead of "soaring."

The Dedalus symbol, then, is rich and many-faceted. Dedalus is a rebel escaping from the labyrinths and nets of authority; he escapes through his own ingenuity; he is maker, artificer. He escapes by flight, in a double sense—in the meaning of "liberation" and of "soaring above." The wings on which he rises are those of the maker, fashioned from "the sluggish matter of the earth" which appears to hold him down. The wings belong to the sense world, though through them the sense world is transcended, and becomes "a new soaring impalpable imperishable being."

## THE STORY PARALLELS THE SYMBOL: FLIGHTS AND CONSTRICTIONS

These elements in the symbol are all paralleled in Stephen's story. He has to rebel from the actualities of contemporary Ireland; the captivity of family, nationality and religion. As he says: "I will not serve that in which I no longer believe, whether it call itself my home, my fatherland or my church." All these are obstructions to his flight. Stephen creates his "wings," as it were, in two ways. On the personal level his intellectual and emotional development fit him finally to assert his own freedom by leaving Ireland; as future artist, he is learning all the time to use *language*, his medium of ingenuity. The new "being" which he finally does create is the book itself, completed ten years after the last events it describes.

The structure of the novel, as critics have pointed out, is in the form of a series of trial flights. At the end of each chapter, Stephen makes some assertion of his own identity which frees him for a time from the particular outer and inner pressures of confusion and despair which constrict him. The diary form at the end of the book, in spite of much of its "flip" tone of cynicism, hints of doubts and wavering distrust. Stephen comments on the story of an old peasant who evidently represents Ireland: "I fear him. . . . It is with him I must struggle all through this night till day come." Torn with conflicting emotions about the girl, who also typifies Ireland, he dismisses them: "O, give it up, old chap! Sleep it off!" To his mother's prayer that in his self-banishment he may learn "what the heart is and what it feels," he acquiesces indifferently: "Amen. So be it." But the final words are exultant:

> Welcome, O life! I go to encounter for the millionth time the reality of experience and to forge in the smithy of my soul the uncreated conscience of my race.

Then the simple invocation:

> Old father, old artificer, stand me now and ever in good stead.

The "conscience of his race" as it appears in the world of his own childhood and adolescence and youth is uniformly corrupt and brutal. Even in the little prelude giving impressionistic glimpses of his earliest memories, *fear* of authority is one element in the atmosphere—"He hid under the table"—and the only way to escape cruel punishment is to submit: "Pull out his eyes,/Apologise." The little boy is surrounded by adults with rigid readymade standards of all conduct and values, and he must conform. At Clongowes external reality shapes itself into a world of unintelligible and confusing codes, of secret guilt and vague sins, of a mob of shouting, pushing fellow creatures, "the whirl of the scrimmage," of snobbish values—your father must be a magistrate—and of gross injustice whereby you are shouldered into a slimy ditch if you won't consent to swap a little snuffbox for a chestnut. Stephen, however, triumphs over all this in the final sequence, where he is unjustly beaten by the sadistic Father Dolan. His shame and rage drive him to report the cruelty to the rector. He is exonerated; his schoolmates applaud his rebellion and he feels "happy and free."

This is all over very soon. The second chapter telescopes his career to the age of sixteen. Again, in the environment of an uncomprehending family, of casuistical[1] priests, of vulgar, insensitive, tormenting schoolboys, Stephen struggles to keep his identity. He finds himself bombarded with exhortations urging him to be athletic and patriotic, a good son, a "decent fellow" and "a good catholic above all things." His only escape is in daydream. Meanwhile, the demands of his growing body subdue everything else. The experience with the harlot which ends the chapter, though so different from his dreams of romance, is again expressed as a triumph. It is an initiation. The yellow gas flames burn "as if before an altar," the groups of women in the street appear "arrayed as for some rite." With a sense of "joy and relief" he surrenders body and mind to the experience and feels suddenly "strong and fearless and sure of himself."

## JOYCE REPORTS STEPHEN'S
## SPIRITUAL EXPERIENCE WITH IRONY

The natural man reaches a temporary fulfillment here, and in the next chapter the spiritual man—or adolescent rather—prevails. The mature Joyce, who is writing the book, reports with deadpan irony the methods of the church to produce repentance. The sermons, addressed by the Jesuit father to his "dear little brothers in Christ," are the crudest appeal to fear. They describe the physical and mental tortures devised by the infinite love of God for his erring children. Stephen, however, perceives no irony. Under the direct emotional onslaught he feels "a terror of spirit as the hoarse voice of the speaker blew death into his soul." In an agony of self-abasement he seeks confession, and then goes home "holy and happy," assured that this was "not a dream from which he would awake. The past was past."

Stephen throws himself into schemes for spiritual regeneration which are heroic in their aspirations. Joyce is openly ironic as he looks back on his young self and describes some of the absurd disciplines he practiced. At the same time he knows very well that the mysteries of religion and its rituals are akin to those of art. He is not ironic when he speaks of

---

1. related to casuistry, the determination of right and wrong in questions of conduct or conscience by the application of general principles of ethics

Stephen's awe before "the divine gloom and silence wherein dwelt the unseen Paraclete,[2] whose symbols were a dove and a mighty wind . . . the eternal, mysterious secret Being to whom as God, the priests offered up mass once a year, robed in the scarlet of the tongues of fire." The flying figure of the hawklike man and his own "deliverance to the winds" while his soul is "soaring sunward" is the secular parallel to the worship of the Holy Ghost. Yet the priest who suggests he may have a religious vocation is part of the evil "conscience of his race" that threatens him. [Critic] Hugh Kenner has pointed out how the details of this scene are an unspoken comment on the church. The priest stands with his back to the light and the light itself is fading, which makes his head look like a skull. His hands are "slowly dangling and looping the cord of the blind" (making a noose for Stephen's neck). As he goes out, the priest's face seems "a mirthless mask reflecting a sunken day." Only when Stephen has put that vision of the future behind him and has asserted his right to go to the University does the vision of his true vocation come, with its sense of exultant ecstasy.

## PROBLEMS INTERPRETING CHAPTER FIVE

The long last chapter repeats again all the elements in his environment which inspire his rebellion. The feckless, poverty-stricken family, where he is still treated like a child by his mother, while mentally and spiritually he is a complete stranger. As he passes from his home to the water-logged streets, stumbling through wet rubbish and moldering offal, he is conscious only of "the sloth of body and soul" which paralyzes Dublin and "the corruption arising from its earth." His blanket condemnations exclude any political or literary hope for his country, and his descriptions of his fellow students at the University are uniformly unfavorable. They are of a different breed from himself. They have unpleasant looks and unpleasant voices; they use the coarsest and most limited vocabulary: they have no intellectual capacity or curiosity, and are utterly without sensibility or dignity. The teachers are no better. As Stephen sits in the classroom "an odour assailed him of cheerless cellar damp and decay," and a "dull torpor of the soul" looks out from "the pale loveless eyes" of the dean of studies. The religion which

2. the Holy Spirit

dominates everything is now dead to him; he gibes at the Irish church as "the scullery maid of Christendom."

It is difficult to know just what Joyce means us to think of Stephen in this chapter. He completed the book when he was a mature man of thirty-two, yet there is little to suggest that he does not regard the priggish and egocentric Stephen with full approval. No doubt by the time he was writing the end of the book, he had *Ulysses* in mind, and knew that Stephen's next appearance would reveal the emptiness of his prideful self-complacency, and that there he would appear as Icarus, "sea-bedabbled, fallen, weltering." But this final chapter gives no hint of that double vision, so well illustrated in [George Eliot's novel] *The Mill on the Floss,* by which maturity can create youth in all its rawness and yet suggest a further adult standard of judgment. Stephen emerges as a most unattractive figure. We sympathize deeply with him in his despair at his temporal conditions: "the life of his body, ill-clad, ill-fed, louse-eaten," and all the humiliations of his miserable poverty and lonely ambitions. We understand that his defensive arrogance springs from inner insecurity. At the same time, except for the one little scene where he pities his brothers and sisters, Stephen has no humility, no generosity, no warmth of heart. He is simply the innocent victim of a hostile environment. He has nothing but scorn for all his fellows; the only person he approves of is himself.

Yet perhaps Joyce's intention may be to suggest that these unpleasant, self-centered qualities in his young self are what made it *possible* for him to take the necessary step toward exile. To all Cranly's moving pleas of human ties and responsibilities he answers stubbornly, "I have to go." His calling as artist demands it and he must serve that vocation.

## STRUGGLES BETWEEN ENVIRONMENT AND INNER LIFE

All through the book Stephen's struggles with his external conventional environment is fused with the development of his own inner life. Toward his surroundings (except at the time of his religious conversion) he is first in unconscious, then in fully conscious, revolt. At the same time, however, he has been shaping a positive identity of his own in "silence, exile and cunning." From the first he possesses the artist's abnormal acuteness to sense impressions. At Clongowes the sensations of cold and wet and darkness particularly assail him, or the "no-coloured" cruel eyes of Father Dolan and the terrible *sound* of the pandybat as it descends. At the same time the memory of colored flowers blots out the misery of doing sums, peasants have a lovely smell of "air and rain and turf and corduroy," and the sound of the cricket bats is "like drops of water in a fountain falling softly in a brimming bowl." Besides all the bombardment of his external senses, he learns one all-important fact: that if he closes the flaps of his ears he can shut out the noise of the refectory and listen to what is going on in his own head. More important still is the discovery that words are as full of mystery as experience in the actual world and are inextricably bound up with it. The same word "belt" can mean different things; the expression "a toe in the rump" is not "nice" and must not be repeated; some words, like "suck," have an ugly sound, but others are "sad and beautiful, like music"; others, like "wine," are full of suggestions, of purple grapes growing outside houses in Greece like white temples.

As he grows older the worlds of reality and dream clash more openly. He continues to learn words avidly, even if he does not yet understand their meaning, or assigns wrong meanings to them. He weaves a romantic ambiance by identifying himself with the hero of *The Count of Monte Cristo*, but is jolted out of that when he finds he is too timid to kiss the willing E—— C—— on the tram. Next day, however, as he tries to write a poem to her, he becomes imaginative artist: ". . . by dint of brooding on the incident, he thought himself into confidence," while "all those elements which he deemed common and insignificant fell out of the scene." Several years later, when he writes his villanelle,[3] the same "enchantment of the heart" pervades him. A "rose and ardent light" glows around, sending forth rays of rhyme and rhythm. On his table is a dirty soup plate and the candle "with its tendrils of tallow"; on his bed his lumpy pillow; outside, life will awaken to "common noises, hoarse voices, sleepy prayers." But he, cowled in his blanket, inhabits the world of creative memory and reverie, while "the liquid letters of speech, symbols of the element of mystery, flowed forth over his brain."

Throughout, the language he hears around him offends his mind and his ear: the "drawling jargon" exchanged by the whores; "a heavy lumpish phrase" used by Cranly,

3. a nineteen-line poem with a fixed form

which sinks "like a stone through a quagmire" and depresses his heart as he compares its quality with either "rare phrases of Elizabethan England" or quaintly turned Irish peasant idioms. As he roams the Dublin streets, musing on [British writer John Henry] Newman's prose or the poetry of Guido Cavalcanti or Ben Jonson and reading "shop legends," he feels he is walking "among heaps of dead language." They are part of the labyrinths he must escape from.

### STEPHEN'S—AND JOYCE'S—THEORY OF ART

In the last chapter Stephen propounds an aesthetic theory which has been much written about. It seems unnecessary to take most of this very seriously. It is Stephen's adolescent theory and is therefore dramatically appropriate, but much of it has, as his friend Lynch remarks coarsely, "the true scholastic stink." Passages read more like a textbook of aesthetics than the living creed of a revolutionary writer. Moreover, Stephen himself repudiates it, saying: "When we come to the phenomena of artistic conception, artistic gestation and artistic reproduction, I require a new terminology and a new personal experience.". . .

As Stephen describes the making of his villanelle he cries: "O! in the virgin womb of the imagination the word was made flesh." Inspiration is an annunciation; the conception and creation of the work of art is an incarnation in which "the sluggish matter of the earth" is united with spirit to produce the miracle of "the word." Again, using what he calls "the radiant image of the Eucharist," Stephen describes himself as "a priest of eternal imagination, transmuting the daily bread of experience into the radiant body of everlasting life."

This "radiance" is the quality Joyce particularly stresses in his theory of art. He translates Aquinas' definition of beauty—*integritas, consonantia, claritas*—as "wholeness, harmony and radiance." *Integritas,* the unity of the work, and *consonantia,* the relationship of its parts, are defined in traditional terms, but his interpretation of *claritas* as "radiance" and his further definition of it as "the scholastic *quidditas,* the *whatness* of a thing," its essence, is his own. . . .

"Radiance" is an excellent word for it, since it suggests its artistic value in two ways. First, it *lights up* the external action or object so that its inner emotion is revealed; and then it extends the meaning so that it *radiates* from the words and images and rhythms. The concluding scenes of the first three chapters are good examples, but it is behind the intensity which Joyce injects throughout into quite minor episodes, such as the child Stephen's discovery of the word *Foetus*[4] cut in the desk of some forgotten medical student at Cork, or the conversation with the Jesuit dean of studies as he is lighting the fire, or the flight of the birds outside the library, or the vision when he sees all his teachers transformed into buffoons.

More complex than any other is the description of the figure of the girl on the beach after the vision of "the hawklike man flying sunward above the sea," and the suggestion of all the emotional associations which radiate from the glimpse of her.

> A girl stood before him in midstream: alone and still, gazing out to sea. She seemed like one whom magic had changed into the likness of a strange and beautiful seabird. Her long slender bare legs were delicate as a crane's and pure save where an emerald trail of seaweed had fashioned itself as a sign upon the flesh. . . . Her slateblue skirts were kilted boldly about her waist and dovetailed behind her. Her bosom was as a bird's, soft and slight, slight and soft as the breast of some dark-plumaged dove. But her long fair hair was girlish: and girlish, and touched with the wonder of mortal beauty, her face.

Stephen has just experienced the certitude of his vocation as artist, and this strange and beautiful figure is a symbol of this. She is Stephen's Muse, as it were. She is mysterious, for all such spiritual revelations rest on mystery. She is birdlike, for the message has come to him from the sky in the symbol of flight. She is a seabird, standing in the flowing waters of life. She is also associated with the dove, bringing to mind the Christian stories of the Annunciation, and the descent of the Holy Ghost—the gift of tongues. Her blue skirts are Mary's color: she is the mother of the Word. But Venus, goddess of beauty, had her doves too, and the pagan symbolism of Venus rising from the sea and being welcomed from the air is there too. (We think of Botticelli's famous painting.) The seaweed, though, making its sign on her flesh, is emerald: she is also Ireland, the emerald isle. She is Stephen's own race, whose uncreated conscience he will forge. She is also Woman, "mortal beauty," for it is from the mortal matter of the earth that the artist creates the immortal word which shall not die.

4. or fetus, meaning in Latin pregnant

Her image had passed into his soul for ever and no word had
broken the holy silence of his ecstasy. Her eyes had called
him and his soul had leaped at the call. To live, to err, to fall,
to triumph, to recreate life out of life! . . . On and on and on
and on!

This is the radiant image of his inspiration as it appeared
to young Stephen as a romantic adolescent, and it is written
in the language of romantic ecstasy.

# Christian Symbolism in *A Portrait*

## C.G. Anderson

C.G. Anderson addresses the complexity of Joyce's symbolism, defining his symbols as expressions of something invisible that deepen and expand meaning. To illustrate, he elaborates the symbolism of the poet as God. Specifically, he likens Stephen's actions to conversion, baptism, and ordination as a priest, and even suggests that Stephen is a Christ figure who participates in the Last Supper. C.G. Anderson taught English at the University of Minnesota. He is the author of the book *James Joyce and His World* and of articles published in the *James Joyce Quarterly* and editor of the Viking Critical Edition of Joyce's *Portrait*.

In everything he [Joyce] wrote after *Stephen Hero* he treated his subject symbolically. The distinction is, as [Irish poet William Butler] Yeats says in *Ideas of Good and Evil*, that while "a symbol is indeed the only possible expression of some invisible essence . . . allegory is one of many possible representations of an embodied thing, or familiar principle, and belongs to fancy and not to imagination: the one is a revelation, the other an amusement." Nevertheless, on the reader's part some allegorizing is necessary if he is to understand how a symbolic work achieves its effect.

Chapter V of the *Portrait* is controlled by three principal symbols: the Daedalus myth; the poet as God—creator, redeemer, and priest; and the betrayal-crucifixion. In addition to subsuming many lesser symbols, these three are themselves related. While Icarus in the Daedalus story is an analogue for the flight of the artist from home, nation, and church into exile, "old father, old artificer" Daedalus corresponds to God the Father and Creator. God the Father is united with Christ the Son, who as the Word joins in cre-

Excerpted from "The Sacrificial Butter," by C.G. Anderson, in *Joyce's* Portrait: *Criticisms and Critiques*, edited by Thomas E. Connolly (New York: Appleton-Century-Crofts, 1962). Reprinted with permission from the author.

ation and as the first priest becomes a creator in Joyce's special sense. Christ, the Creator as a young man, is betrayed and crucified in a way which corresponds to the betrayal of the artist as a young man by his family, his national society, and his church. Since the Daedalus element has been, in general, clear from the beginning, this article will examine only the second and third of these principal symbols.

Stephen's exposition of his esthetic to Lynch in Chapter V is the intellectual climax of the novel. Stephen is here an ordained priest of art proclaiming the gospel of art. As he says of himself, he is ". . . a priest of eternal imagination, transmuting the daily bread of experience into the radiant body of everliving life." But to understand his priesthood, we must understand his conversion and baptism.

### STEPHEN'S SYMBOLIC CONVERSION AND BAPTISM

When, in Chapter IV, the director of University College suggests that Stephen consider becoming a Jesuit, Stephen decides that he will ". . . never swing the thurible before the altar as priest." But later, as he walks along the beach, he hears ". . . the call of life to his soul not the dull gross voice of the world of duties and despair, not the inhuman voice that had called him to the pale service of the altar." He is born again, and his soul arises from the ". . . grave of boyhood, spurning her graveclothes." He feels that his calling and election are sure, and he immediately accepts his vocation: "Yes! Yes! Yes! He would create proudly out of the freedom and power of his soul . . . a living thing, new and soaring and beautiful, impalpable, imperishable."

Stephen is baptized by wading in the sea, and he feels the regenerative power of this sacrament. He feels ". . . a new wild life . . . singing in his veins" and wonders, "Where was his boyhood now? Where was the soul that had hung back from her destiny to brood alone upon the shame of her wounds . . . ?"[1]

At the opening of Chapter V Stephen already has passed from baptism through ordination, and is saying mass. Contrasting with the Shelleyan[2] swoon of the baptism and its ecstatic aftermath in the final pages of Chapter IV, the first

---

1. During his baptism Stephen sees the wading figure of a girl—symbol of the fleshly beauty to which he has been converted, and symbol of Emma—on whom ". . . an emerald trail of sea-weed had fashioned itself as a sign upon the flesh." Because she is baptized—chosen and marked with the sign—he sees her as a bird capable of flying with the "hawklike man," although ultimately she becomes the "batlike soul" who cannot soar with Icarus.    2. referring to the style of poet Percy Bysshe Shelley

sentence of Chapter V is a rhetorical change of pace: "He drained his third cup of watery tea to the dregs and set to chewing the crusts of fried bread that were scattered near him, staring into the dark pool of the jar."

## STEPHEN PRIEST AND THE MAUNDY THURSDAY MASS

Important as this deflation is to the stylistic structure of the novel, however, the sentence is at least as important because it introduces the symbol of the eucharist—specifically, as we shall see, of the eucharist in the Maundy Thursday Mass. The tea and bread are paralleled by the cocoa which Stephen drinks with Bloom in the cabmen's shelter and at 7 Eccles Street in the Eumaeus and Ithaca episodes of *Ulysses.* After Stephen has consumed his breakfast of bread and tea (read bread and wine), he takes up ". . . idly one after another the blue and white dockets. . . ." of his pawn brokers. These represent the communion wafers. After he has fingered them, he puts them aside and gazes ". . . thoughtfully at the lid of the box [i.e., the tabernacle] speckled with louse marks." Then his sister Maggie, representing the acolyte of the mass, prepares the water for the purification of his fingers, a ceremony which follows directly after, the second ablution in the mass.

As is usual with Joyce, things are not so simple as they appear at second glance. Stephen's mother washes his neck. Because the reader already knows that Stephen has abhorred water since childhood and has lice, he realizes at once that this is a rather singular endeavor; it is not an ordinary Ordinary[3] of the mass, but one which, no doubt has its Proper of the Season.[4] What this Proper is, however, and what symbolic meaning it has, is discovered more gradually. Although Joyce knows very well what day it is, Stephen and the reader do not learn that it is Thursday until Stephen reads a news-agent's placard as he walks to school. Thursday is the day which Stephen in his earlier Catholic fervor had dedicated to the Most Blessed Sacrament. And later, when Stephen refers to St. Thomas' *Pange lingua gloriosi,* he mentions to Lynch, who knows the fact as well as he does, that it is "a hymn for Maundy Thursday." The Maundy Thursday Communion Verse, which follows the Purification in the order of the mass liturgy, says that ". . . the Lord Jesus, after He had supped

---

3. a part of the mass that remains from day to day    4. one used in the liturgy of a particular feast or season of the year

with His disciples, washed their feet." Stephen ". . . allowed his mother to scrub his neck and root into the folds of his ears and into the interstices at the wings of his nose," and we are reminded that Peter, in the Maundy Thursday Gospel, when he consents to Christ's washing him at all, says, "Lord, not my feet, but my hands also, and my head."

After Stephen as priest has purified his fingers, his mother as server thrusts ". . . a damp overall into his hands, saying:—Dry yourself and hurry out for the love of goodness." The overall, which represents the priest's napkin, is damp at the Purification because it has already been used in the Washing-of-the-Hands ceremony during the Offertory of the mass. The hurry and the return of Stephen's sister ". . . making signs to him to be quick and go out quietly by the back" suggest the hustle of the final portion of the mass. Stephen gives the Benediction by ". . . smiling and kissing the tips of his fingers adieu." But at least two other meanings are compressed into this single ironic action. It is the priest wiping his lips and the priest kissing the altar before he pronounces the Benediction.

As Stephen leaves the house he hears the mad nun in the nearby asylum screech, "Jesus! Jesus! Jesus!" Her exclamation is in the correct mouth and in the correct ritualistic context to signify the thanksgiving of an individual madwoman for the mad sacrament of a mad service. But it also identifies Stephen with Christ, the first priest. That this identification is what Joyce is actually saying is borne out later in the chapter when the Maundy Thursday symbol is made more explicit by the consideration which Stephen and Lynch give to St. Thomas' *Pange lingua gloriosi* and to the *Vexilla Regis* of Venantius Fortunatus. . . .

## THE LITURGY AS SYMBOL

The two hymns are of primary importance in understanding Joyce's method of using liturgy as symbol. The first hymn is merely named and called the "highest glory of the hymnal." But, Stephen says, ". . . there is no hymn that can be put beside that mournful and majestic processional song, the *Vexilla Regis.* . . ." Lynch then sings a stanza of the second hymn from memory. In the liturgy the *Pange lingua gloriosi* is sung after the mass on Maundy Thursday, when the second Host,[5]

5. the consecrated bread or wafer of the Eucharist

which has been consecrated to be reserved for the Good Friday Mass in which no consecration takes place, is carried in procession to the chapel or some other place. When the procession arrives at this place, the chalice [*sic*] containing the Host is incensed and placed in an urn or tabernacle. The procession then returns, and Vespers are sung in the choir. The *Vexilla Regis* is the hymn for Vespers during Passiontide.

The discussion of the hymns interrupts Stephen's expounding of the mysteries of art to Lynch, and they are by no means used merely to complete a parody or to give relief from what might have become an esthetically tedious exposition of an esthetic. The line *Pange lingua gloriosi* is translated in the Missal as "Now, my tongue the mystery telling"; and Lynch does not sing the first stanza of the *Vexilla Regis*, which begins in translation with "Behold the royal ensigns fly," but the second stanza, beginning "The mystery we now unfold." The hymns as symbol, therefore—and this is true of all Joyce's symbols—are not used as mere decoration, nor as extraneous allegorical signs; the meanings they add to the narrative are intimately important to the narrative, giving it depth of texture and expansiveness. It is important that we know that Stephen is expounding mysteries, but it is also important that we know he is expounding them in his symbolic office as Stephen-Christ, the first priest of art.

When Lynch has finished singing, he and Stephen turn into Lower Mount Street. As we shall see this may be connected with Golgotha, for when they stop the crucifixion is re-enacted; but one of its other connections is the prophecy which Stephen made when he accepted the call to the religion of art in Chapter IV: ". . . dawn . . . [would] show him strange fields and hills and faces." Here is the hill, and Donovan's bloated face appears.

## THE SYMBOLIC LAST SUPPER

Stephen and Lynch halt their procession; and although it is still Thursday on the narrative level, the conversation with Donovan symbolically treats the Last Supper in retrospect. This is important because of the re-enactment of the crucifixion which is to take place shortly. Telling of a group of students (read disciples) who have passed their examination successfully, Donovan says, "The Irish fellows in Clark's gave them a feed last night. They all ate curry." These students are apostles ready to go forth to all nations: "Halpin and O'Flynn are through the home civil. Moonan got fifth place in the Indian."

Food continues to be the controlling image in their conversation. Stephen asks Donovan twice to bring him "a few turnips and onions" the next time he goes on a botany field trip so that he can "make a stew;" Donovan mentions that his sister is to make pancakes for supper; and Lynch expresses disgust that pancake-eating Donovan can get a good job while he has to smoke cheap cigarettes.

Stephen ends the delineation of his esthetic with the now famous statement, "The artist, like the God of creation, remains within or behind or beyond or above his handiwork, invisible, refined out of existence, indifferent, paring his fingernails." The artist is God; God is Jesus; Stephen is Jesus. As Jesus left the companionship of his disciples on Maundy Thursday for the exile of the cross and the grave, Stephen is leaving Lynch, his pope, and Emma, his Blessed Virgin, as well as his family, nation, and church for the exile of the artist and for Paris.

# The Underlying Structure of *A Portrait*'s Episodes

Richard F. Peterson

Richard F. Peterson imposes an orderly chronology on *A Portrait*'s sporadic episodes. Though years may pass between episodes, the action of chapters 1 and 2 follows the progression of the seasons. In some instances time passes according to body rhythms and the regular rhythm of the tide, and many episodes correspond to feast days celebrated through the church year. Peterson notes that time pauses in chapter 4 but resumes its advance in chapter 5 according to church festivals and regular schedules. Richard F. Peterson has taught English at Southern Illinois University at Carbondale. He is the author of *Mary Levin, William Butler Yeats,* and articles on Irish literature published in *Modern Fiction Studies, Studies in Short Fiction, Éire-Ireland,* and the *James Joyce Quarterly.*

While Stephen's experiences in the first chapter appear to leap forward fitfully because of the impressionistic style and structure of *A Portrait*, there is a definite and separate pattern to the episodes that give the chapter a good measure of its unity and balance. Though there is a gap of several months between each major experience in Stephen's life, we have the chance to observe a season-by-season movement from episode to episode. The first impression of Stephen's life at Clongowes is cloaked in the dampness and gloom of the early October days of 1891. Stephen, "caught in the whirl of a scrimmage" of footballers, anticipates changing the number pasted up inside his desk from seventy-seven to seventy-six (the days remaining before the holiday), and

Excerpted from "Stephen and the Narrative of *A Portrait of the Artist as a Young Man*," by Richard F. Peterson, in *Work in Progress: Joyce Centenary Essays,* edited by Richard F. Peterson, Alan M. Cohn, and Edmund L. Epstein. Copyright ©1983 by the Board of Trustees, Southern Illinois University. Reprinted by permission of the publisher.

dreams of Parnell's[1] body being returned to Dublin. In the second episode, the narrative advances to Christmas as the scene shifts to Stephen's first Christmas Day dinner at his father's table. The holiday anticipated at Clongowes is now clearly identified and the reason for the vividness of Parnell's death in Stephen's mind is underscored by the content of the quarrel at the dinner table. In the final episode, the second at Clongowes, the seasonal pattern of the chapter is definitely established. While Stephen shares in the atmosphere of fear, he notices that "there was no play on the football grounds for cricket was coming." Shortly after the pandying, he finds that he "could not eat the blackish fish fritters they got on Wednesdays in Lent," and after his visit to the rector, he sees that the "fellows were practising long shies and bowing lobs and slow twisters." Thus, while Stephen undergoes three experiences that momentarily bewilder his sense of the proper order of things and form an early chain of events that will lead to his decision to become the artist, the world around him asserts its separate reality as the seasons advance from fall to winter to spring. As Stephen moves toward the moment when he discovers his soul and the nature in which he will express his discovery, the early narrative pattern of *A Portrait* gives to the impending moment an air of inevitability.

## THE SEASONS IN CHAPTER TWO

Before Stephen discovers his soul, however, he learns through another fitful series of disturbing and painful impressions that he has a body. The advancing tide of Stephen's puberty and the winding journey in the second chapter from Mercedes to E—— C—— and finally to the prostitute is also apprehended within a definite movement of the seasons. Even though several years have elapsed since Stephen's crisis of authority, the seasons hold to their own pattern as Stephen now feels the first stirrings of sexuality. As Stephen endured the humiliation of the pandying in the early spring, so he now pores over his ragged translation of *The Count of Monte Cristo* and becomes a leader of a gang of adventurous youths during "the first part of the summer." The "coming of September" fails to trouble him this year because he is not

---

1. Charles Stewart Parnell was a member of Parliament from 1875, a supporter of Home Rule for Ireland. He died in 1891.

being sent to Clongowes. Shortly after, the Dedalus family moves to the city of Dublin, Stephen observes the "jovial array of shops lit up and adorned for Christmas," and attends a party at Harold's Cross. When he learns that his father has made arrangements for him at Belvedere the season appears to be turning once again.

The next time we see Stephen he is now firmly set in the pattern of Belvedere life. The Whitsuntide play in which he has the chief role of the farcical pedagogue takes place during his second year at the Jesuit day school. There is another leap in the narrative, this time nearly two years, but the seasons still pass in their natural order. While Stephen talks to Heron and his friend just before the beginning of the play, he remembers "a raw spring morning" toward the end of his first term at Belvedere when he was accused of heresy in his essay, and, a few nights later, was abused by Heron and two other youths after he defended Byron as a better poet than Tennyson. This memory clearly establishes the season when Stephen learns from his father that he is being sent to Belvedere, and places that scene within a deliberate narrative pattern that has advanced in the present episode to late spring since Whitsuntide week begins on the seventh Sunday after Easter.

When Stephen visits Cork with his father, he is conscious of the summer atmosphere of the "warm sunny city" and the whispering leaves of the blooming trees that speak to the fever in his blood. In the next episode, the seasons advance again as a "keen October wind" cuts through the figure of Stephen's thinly clad mother on the family's way from the bank of Ireland with the exhibition and essay prize money. When an artificial and all too "swift season of merrymaking" fails to stay the relentless decline of the family's fortune or the brutal urgings of his body, Stephen prowls the streets during the "veiled autumnal evenings" until he finally surrenders in a swoon into the arms of a prostitute.

By the end of the second chapter, Stephen has experienced two major crises and his life has advanced several years in the process. While Stephen's early ordeals have been presented through a series of rapidly moving, almost fitful impressions, the narrative has carefully recorded the passing of the seasons. In the last three chapters of *A Portrait*, the impressions of Stephen's life do not move as rapidly within the context of each chapter or from chapter to chapter because of the approaching moment of discovery and decision in his life, but the narrative still gives the world around Stephen its own separate reality.

## THE MOVEMENT OF TIME AND THE TIDES

Two other patterns have also emerged by the end of the second chapter to reinforce the idea of external reality in *A Portrait*. While the seasons have passed in their inexorable order, we have also had the chance to hear and feel time moving along its inevitable course, even though clocks never actually tick in the early chapters. At the end of the first chapter, Stephen experiences the first thrill of being alone and free, but when the cheers of the students die away, he hears "through the quiet air the sound of the cricket bats: pick, pack, pock, puck: like drops of water in a fountain falling softly in the brimming bowl." In the second chapter, the association of time and water becomes more pronounced. As Stephen struggles with his growing sexuality, he feels his heart dancing like "a cork upon a tide." And when he finally admits his failure "to build a breakwater of order and elegance against the sordid tide of life without him," he also recognizes that he is incapable of damming "the powerful recurrence of the tides within him."

## THE PROGRESS OF CHURCH HOLIDAYS

While time and the body's rhythm, associated with the movement of the tides, advance ineluctably through the early chapters, another pattern, reflective of the human desire to give a special order and religious meaning to experience, emerges in *A Portrait*. In each of the first two chapters, a feast day of the Church is the focal point of Stephen's crisis. The violent political quarrel takes place at Christmas, a day invested not only with great religious meaning but one that has taken on a special significance for Stephen because it represents his first school holiday and his first Christmas dinner with his mother and father. In the second chapter, Stephen endures his greatest frustration and remembers his worst humiliation on the evening of the Whitsuntide play. While the play itself has a Pentecostal effect upon Stephen, briefly returning him to the innocent mirth of boyhood, his painful memory of the beating and his frustrated anticipation of meeting the girl of his secret desires jar his nerves and increase the riot in his blood to the point that only the rank odor of horse piss and rotted straw can calm him—for the moment.

At the beginning of the third chapter, the seasons appear about to continue their separate and inevitable pace. The "veiled autumnal evenings" that found Stephen prowling through nighttown have now advanced to the days followed by the "swift December dusk." There are, however, no great chronological leaps within the chapter. Instead, the narrative is limited to the few days of Stephen's spiritual trial. Stephen discovers the mortal dangers to his soul during the retreat in honor of Saint Francis Xavier's feast day, which is celebrated on the third day in December. Most of the chapter takes place from Wednesday, when Father Arnall begins his fiery sermon, to Saturday, the feast day of Saint Francis, when Stephen receives holy communion and believes that he has overcome the urgings of his body by returning in spirit to the innocence of boyhood: "Another life! A life of grace and virtue and happiness! It was true. It was not a dream from which he would wake. The past was past."

In the third chapter, then, while Stephen is undergoing that "slow and dark birth" of the soul he describes in a later scene with Lynch, the narrative appears to slow down and the seasons seem to pause at their darkest moment. The feast day of the Church, rather than appearing in passing as it did in the earlier chapters, occurs at the end of the chapter, thereby seeming to bring some sense of spiritual climax to Stephen's life. His sins trickle from his lips at confession "in shameful drops from his soul festering and oozing like a sore, a squalid stream of vice," thereby seeming to bring to an end the rhythm of Stephen's development.

If there was ever any doubt, however, that Stephen's destiny in *A Portrait* is bound by environment and experience, the beginning of the fourth chapter quickly dispels it. Though Stephen's life is still dominated by the religious life and his days are measured by the Church calendar—"Sunday was dedicated to the mystery of the Holy Trinity, Monday to the Holy Ghost, Tuesday . . ." the narrative again asserts its separate reality. The seasons still fall within a perceivable pattern and the flowing rhythm of Stephen's life, which appeared to trickle to a stop during the retreat, resumes its natural course. During the winter and approaching spring of Stephen's amended life, he feels, in spite of his scrupulous religious habits, "a flood slowly advancing towards his naked feet" and waits "for the first faint timid noiseless wavelet to touch his fevered skin." In the waning hours of "the long summer daylight," Stephen finally hears and knows he will reject the offer to study for the priesthood because he recognizes that after "so many years of order and obedience" he will now resist any effort of priest or his own "to end for ever, in time and in eternity, his freedom."

## A CHANGE OF PACE IN THE FINAL TWO CHAPTERS

There is an apparent pause in the narrative movement at the end of the fourth chapter, but the suspended moment of Stephen's epiphany, unlike the perverse attempt to defy experience in the previous chapter, is in perfect harmony with external reality. Stephen's discovery of his artistic mission, of the potential form in which his soul will express itself, shines forth in time and eternity. Knowing that he will never become a priest of the Church, he decides, at this supreme moment of his youth, to "create proudly out of the freedom and power of his soul, as the great artificer whose name he bore, a living thing, new and soaring and beautiful, impalpable, imperishable."

A year has elapsed since the summer day before the start of Stephen's last year at Belvedere when he was offered the secret knowledge and power of the priesthood, but summer remains the season for Stephen's epiphany, which occurs just after he learns that he will be entering the university. The rhythmic pattern of tides that has reinforced and corresponded to the seasonal movement in *A Portrait* and, at times, even challenged Stephen during his moments of crisis and development now seems to surrender to Stephen's profound vision, which shines forth in the image of the seagirl he encounters while wading in a rivulet of the receding tidal waters. Stephen's epiphany, delivered out of the virgin womb of his own imagination, replaces the feast day of the Church and unfolds itself in the Dantean imagery of the soul as a wave-like flower spreading "in endless succession to itself, breaking in full crimson and unfolding and fading to palest rose, leaf by leaf and wave of light by wave of light, flooding all the heavens with its soft flushes, every flush deeper than the other."

The brief pause in the narrative of *A Portrait*, as the soul discovers and celebrates its own self-sustaining rhythm, underlines the crucial importance of Stephen's epiphany, but it does not negate the importance of the world around him. At the moment when Stephen finally sees the potential of his soul in an image of beauty, he appears in perfect harmony with all that surrounds him. In other words, Stephen's vision appears transcendental, suspended beyond time because of its radiance and pristine source, but it is actualized within Stephen's world of experience—a truth Stephen will struggle against in *Ulysses* as he tries to reconcile the artist's imagination and the too often nightmarish reality of his life.

In the last chapter of *A Portrait* the narrative, now that Stephen's radiant vision has faded, assumes its separate course again. Rather than appearing to be in harmony with Stephen's soul, the narrative pattern now reinforces the ironic mode of the chapter by exposing Stephen's poverty and immaturity. Thus within the narrative frame of *A Portrait*, while Stephen may discover the true nature of his soul and know that his destiny is to express his discovery in artistic form, *A Portrait* ends with Stephen still a young man. While most of the final chapter, like the third and fourth, takes place within a few days, the narrative has already advanced through the disillusionment of the autumn and winter of Stephen's university career. We see him at the beginning of the chapter walking within a world of "rainladen trees" and "the strange wild smell of the wet leaves and bark" that contrasts sharply with the squalor and confusion of his home. Now that Stephen possesses the knowledge of his soul, he resists the world more than ever, but, like it or not, his life still advances along its irresistible course, and the Church, which Stephen claims to serve no longer, still has its own order which acts insistently upon Stephen's life.

The narrative pattern now clearly exposes Stephen's dilemma at the end of *A Portrait*. While Stephen rejects the life of his family, nation, and religion and holds his knowledge of the true nature of his soul and destiny above the world around him, his Dublin life continues its inevitable movement and, accordingly, the feast days of the Church fall within their appointed pattern. Stephen may move to the rhythm of his own imagination, but the English class begins at ten whether he is there or not.

# CHAPTER 3

# The Characterization of Stephen Dedalus

# Stephen Dedalus and Women

Suzette Henke

Suzette Henke traces the process by which Stephen first acquires impressions of feminine and masculine roles during childhood and then learns that his mother is powerless to protect him from a tough, masculine world. In the course of the novel, Henke argues, Stephen rejects various images of women and ultimately rejects women and feminine qualities altogether and adopts a masculine role of order and law. The narcissism and misogyny that characterize his masculine image are traits that hamper his ability to become a mature artist, according to Henke. Suzette Henke teaches literary studies at the University of Louisville in Kentucky. She is the author of *Joyce's Moraculous Sindbook: A Study of "Ulysses"* and *James Joyce and the Politics of Desire.*

Female characters are present everywhere and nowhere in *A Portrait of the Artist as a Young Man.* They pervade the novel, yet remain elusive. Their sensuous figures haunt the developing consciousness of Stephen Dedalus and provide a foil against which he defines himself as both man and artist. Like everything else in *A Portrait*, women are portrayed almost exclusively from Stephen's point of view. Seen through his eyes and colored by his fantasies, they often appear as one-dimensional projections of a narcissistic imagination. Demonized by Stephen's childhood sense of abjection,[1] women emerge as powerful emblems of the flesh—frightening reminders of sex, generation, and bodily decay.

## STEPHEN'S FIRST MALE-FEMALE IMPRESSIONS

At the dawn of infantile consciousness, Stephen interprets the external world in terms of complementary pairs: male

1. of the lowest, most miserable condition or status

and female, father and mother, politics and religion, Davitt and Parnell. Baby Stephen's cosmos is organized in binary structures that set the stage for a dialectic of personal development. He perceives his father as a primordial storyteller who inaugurates the linguistic apprenticeship that inscribes the boy into the symbolic order of patriarchal authority. Simon Dedalus is a bearer of the law and the word, twin instruments of the will that promise psychological mastery over a hostile material environment. The male parent appeals to Stephen's imagination, awakening him to a sense of individual identity at the moment when language necessarily establishes a gap between subjective desire and self-representation: "He was baby tuckoo. . . . He sang that song. That was his song." By virtue of receiving a forename, Stephen is able to enunciate himself as a subject of discourse and to gain access to narrative representation. Inscribed into the linguistic circuit of exchange, he identifies himself in terms of the dominant culture's signifying practices.

At the psychological juncture between pre-oedipal[2] attachment and oedipal separation, Stephen first sees his mother as a powerful and beneficent source of physical pleasure. She ministers to her son's corporal needs, changes the oilsheet, and encourages his artistic expression by playing the piano. This sweet-smelling guardian is more directly responsive to the boy's infantile emotional demands and more closely associated with sensuous comfort and bodily joy. It is the "nice" mother, however, whom Stephen recognizes as one of the women principally responsible for introducing him to a hostile external world and to the repressive strictures of middle-class morality. The first of the many imperatives that thwart his ego, "apologise," is associated in his mind and vivid imagination with matriarchal threats.

## STEPHEN'S INITIATION INTO THE STRUGGLE FOR DOMINANCE AND POWER

The sexual antagonism that pervades Irish society is impressed on Stephen at an early age. He loathes his mother's feminine vulnerability and thinks that she is "not nice" when she bursts into tears. Armed with ten shillings and his

---

2. Psychoanalyst Sigmund Freud referred to the Oedipus complex: a boy's passion for his mother generates feelings of desire and pleasure but also of guilt and fear.

father's injunction toward a code of masculine loyalty, he enters the competitive joust of life at Clongowes determined to adopt an ethic of manly stoicism: "his father had told him . . . whatever he did, never to peach on a fellow."

In a world of social Darwinism where only the ruthless survive, Stephen defines himself as both literally and figuratively marginal. Small, frail, and feeling very much like an outsider in this thundering herd of pugnacious schoolboys, he mentally takes refuge in artistic evocations of the family hearth protected by beneficent female spirits. As he relives the horror of being shouldered into a rat-infested urinal ditch by the bully Wells, Stephen projects himself beyond the vermin and the scum to an apparently dissociated reverie of his mother sitting by the fire in hot "jewelly slippers" that exude a "lovely warm smell." Alienated from a brutal male environment, Stephen longs to return to this female figure of security and comfort, "to be at home and lay his head on his mother's lap."

As the growing boy moves in the direction of manhood, he feels increasingly compelled to cast off the shackles of female influence. His childhood educator Dante, "a clever woman and a wellread woman" who teaches him geography and lunar lore, is supplanted by male instructors: "Father Arnall knew more than Dante because he was a priest." The Jesuit masters at Clongowes invite Stephen to ponder the mysteries of religion, death, canker, and cancer. They introduce him to a system of male authority and discipline, to a pedagogical regimen that will ensure his correct training and proper socialization. Through examinations that pit red roses against white, Yorks against Lancastrians, they make education an aggressive game of simulated warfare in which students, like soldiers, are depersonalized through institutional surveillance.

## STEPHEN FINDS NO SANCTUARY FROM MALE-DOMINATED STRUCTURE

By the time Stephen is old enough to join his parents' table at Christmas, his mother can no longer protect him from the world of masculine aggression or the turbulence of Irish politics. At the holiday meal, the impressionable child assimilates the knowledge that rabid women like Dante Riordan support ecclesiastical authority in the name of moral righteousness. Like the Irish sow devouring her farrow, Dante is willing to sacrifice Parnell[3] as a political scapegoat to the prelates of Irish Catholicism. In the face of Mr. Casey's Fenianism[4] and Simon's contemptuous snorting, she labels the Catholic clergy "the apple of God's eye." *"Touch them not, says* Christ, *for they are the apple of My eye."* As Ireland's perverted Eve, Dante defends this ecclesiastical apple against an adulterous Nationalist leader, a scandalous sinner crushed by an irate populace. Her impassioned ravings, bred of puritanical self-righteousness, suggest a formidable alliance between the Catholic church and the ideals of bourgeois morality guarded by a horde of pious women. "God and morality and religion come first," shrieks Dante, and Mr. Casey counters with his own incendiary slogan.

In the battle between male and female, Mother Church emerges as a bastion of sexual repression. Dante's own credibility is socially diminished by her age, gender, and involuntary celibacy. Stephen "had heard his father say that she was a spoiled nun and that she had come out of the convent in the Alleghanies when her brother had got the money from the savages for the trinkets and the chainies." Stephen's own role models, Simon Dedalus and John Casey, boldly assert masculine prowess through republican fervor directed against dissenting countrymen rather than their imperial masters. In this mock scenario of political self-assertion, women and children prove fair game. Hence Casey's braggadocio in recounting his triumph over the hag who screamed "whore": "I had my mouth full of the tobacco juice. I bent down to her and *Phth!* says I to her like that . . . right into her eye."

When Stephen returns to Clongowes, he realizes that his peacemaking mother, a mollifying agent of social arbitration, has failed to offer a viable sanctuary from the male-dominated power structure that controls the outer world. He must learn to survive in a society that protects bullies like Wells and sadists like Father Dolan, condones brutality, and takes advantage of the weak and the helpless. The pandybat incident at the end of chapter one symbolically reinforces the rites of objectification characteristic of Jesuit training. Stephen is being socialized into what Philip Slater identifies in *The Glory of Hera* as a culture of male narcissism. Ac-

3. Charles Stewart Parnell was an Irish member of Parliament supporting Home Rule. He died in 1891.    4. The Fenians were a secret revolutionary organization founded in 1858.

cording to Slater, single-sex education and the separation of young boys from maternal nurturance promotes misogyny,[5] narcissism, and a residual terror of the female. Little boys suffer from an "unconscious fear of being feminine, which leads to 'protest masculinity,' exaggeration of the difference between men and women." Once the child is deprived of his mother's affection, he "seeks compensation through self-aggrandizement—renouncing love for admiration. . . . He becomes vain, hypersensitive, invidious, ambitious, boastful, and exhibitionistic."

Stephen's brash appeal to Father Conmee at the end of the episode is motivated not only by optimistic faith in a male-controlled world but by personal vanity and a tendency toward exhibitionism. "The prefect of studies was a priest but that was cruel and unfair," he insists. With an absurdly Panglossian[6] view of the world, he feels certain of ethical exoneration from Conmee. Having rebelled against Father Dolan's totalitarian power, Stephen is unanimously acclaimed a revolutionary hero by his jubilant peers. But the child, apparently triumphant, later discovers an ironic sequel to his ostensible victory: Dolan and Conmee, in smug condescension, treat the incident as a riproaring joke. Stephen has unwittingly played the fool at the court of his Jesuit masters and, in a bold attempt to assert his budding manhood, has merely served as an object of wry patriarchal amusement.

## STEPHEN TRANSFORMS SYMBOLIC WOMAN INTO SYMBOLIC MUSE

In chapter five of *Portrait*, Cranly asks Stephen if he would deflower a virgin. His companion replies by posing another half-mocking query: "Excuse me, . . . is that not the ambition of most young gentlemen?" Figuratively, it is Stephen's ambition throughout the novel to deflower the Blessed Virgin of Catholicism and supplant the Italian Madonna with a profane surrogate—a voluptuous Irish muse rooted in sensuous reality. . . .

The formal, highly wrought verses of the villanelle ingeniously subdue the seductress whose *"eyes have set man's heart ablaze"* from the beginning of time. Against overwhelming enchantment, Stephen arrays the forces of aesthetic transformation. As poet-priest, he transubstantiates the eternal feminine into a disembodied muse that, once out

5. hatred of women 6. blindly or naively optimistic

of nature, ceases to threaten. Consigned to the realm of Byzantium, the Circean[7] figure can no longer arouse animal lust or sensuous desire.

### WOMEN AS MUSE

*In "Joyce and Feminism," Karen Lawrence comments on the curtailed role of women in* A Portrait. *She suggests that women's purpose is more symbolic than actual.*

Joyce himself curtails the role of the female between *Stephen Hero,* the long unpublished novel in which both his mother and Emma Clery have explicit and extended roles, and the much shorter *Portrait.* May Dedalus, whose conversations are recorded in the earlier version of Stephen's story, is deprived of most of her lines and much of her role in *A Portrait.* And, as numerous critics have observed, Emma Clery is transformed from a character with a body and a name, to an object of mystery and intrigue—an ambivalent focus of desire, fear, and friendship whose presence—like the 'characters' of *Finnegans Wake*—is signified by her initials (E.C.).

It is as if the image of the female were abstracted by Joyce so that Stephen must incarnate it himself, for ultimately Stephen seeks to convert abstract beauty and desire into poetry. As he has his 'epiphany' of the bird girl at the end of part IV, Stephen feels 'her image pass into his soul for ever.' But he begins to realize that the image must pass out as well, if he is to be a 'priest of the eternal imagination' and transmute the spirit into a material image. The muse is crucial to this incarnation; somehow it is her spirit that must be embodied. One might say with Molly [in Ulysses] that all poets merely 'want to write about some woman', but the female is more than a topic here; she is projected as the muse of representation, of embodiment. Her image haunts his days and his nights, as he struggles to refine it into poetry.

Derek Attridge, ed., *The Cambridge Companion to James Joyce.* New York: Cambridge University Press, 1990.

Throughout the novel, Stephen seeks the evacuation of affect[8] from language and a reinscription of his filial self into the symbolic order and law of the father. By replicating himself in a discursive process of substitutability, he acquires a

---

7. in Greek mythology Circe is a sorceress who turned Odysseus's men temporarily into swine   8. emotion; feeling

male aesthetic signature and triumphantly appropriates the female body/text. Inscribing himself into an august company of paternal authority figures (Daedalus, Edmond Dantes, Lord Byron, Father Conmee, Father Arnall, Dante Alighieri, Simon Dedalus, and Cranly), he fabricates an authorial persona purged of unsettling libidinal drives. The eternal temptress he celebrates is a disguised replica of the phallic mother who tantalizes with nurturant pleasure, then obstinately withholds satisfaction. Incestuous attraction to the body of the mother is repressed and displaced onto a radiant icon of female beauty. Emma provides a substitute for the mother (both consubstantial and Catholic Madonna) whose image, in turn, is reproduced in the specular icon of a wading bird-girl, then lyrically transformed into an enchantress idealized out of existence and consigned to the icy realm of Platonic stasis.[9]

## STEPHEN FLEES WOMEN AND JOINS MASCULINE FRATERNITY

Through *Portrait*, Stephen manifests a psychological horror of woman as a figure of immanence, a symbol of unsettling sexual difference, and a perpetual reminder of bodily abjection. At the conclusion of chapter five, he prepares to flee from all the women who have served as catalysts in his own adolescent development. His journey into exile will release him from what he perceives as a cloying matriarchal authority. He must blot from his ears "his mother's sobs and reproaches" and strike from his eyes the insistent "image of his mother's face."

Alone and proud, isolated and free, Stephen proclaims joyful allegiance to the masculine fraternity of Daedalus, his priest and patron: "Welcome, O life! I go to encounter for the millionth time the reality of experience and to forge in the smithy of my soul the uncreated conscience of my race."

The hyperbolic resonance of Stephen's invocation leads us to suspect that his fate will prove Icarian rather than Daedalian. Insofar as women are concerned, he goes to encounter the reality of experience not for the millionth time but for the first. Much of the irony in *Portrait* results from Joyce's satirical rendering of Stephen's logocentric paradigm. The sociopathic hero, pompous and aloof, passionately gathers phrases for his word hoard without infusing

9. a condition of balance among various forces; motionlessness

his "capful of light odes" (*Ulysses* 14:1119) with the generative spark of human sympathy.

Certainly, the reader may feel baffled or uneasy about the degree of irony implicit in Joyce's portrait of the artist as a young narcissist. Stephen/Icarus has flown from one youthful illusion to another, first trusting the rectitude of his Clongowes masters and emulating the Count of Monte Cristo, then sliding into illicit sexual exultation in an initiation ritual immediately undercut by scenes of debased sensuality and emotional self-hatred. As the body, in turn, is disciplined and mortified, a devotion to the priesthood of art displaces the young man's Catholic asceticism. Embracing his newfound mission with all the exuberance of an aesthetic convert, Stephen is left exhausted and swooning before the sanctified icon of a wading girl transformed in his imagination into a mystical muse. Incapable of sustaining this romantic fantasy in the hostile environment of Dublin, he takes psychological refuge in vaguely erotic verses generated by a wet dream and/or by masturbatory excitation. Toward the end of the novel, Stephen adopts a Wildean pose of triumphant perversity as he proclaims revolutionary freedom and projects a vision of liberating flight "across the kathartic ocean" (*Finnegans Wake* 185.6) to the haunts of bohemian Paris. Emotionally static and incapable of meaningful connection with other human beings, the aspiring poet is poised in a stance of Icarian impotence. His final diary entries suggest imminent emigration, but they delineate neither flight nor failure.

## THE SIGNIFICANCE OF STEPHEN'S NARCISSISM AND MISOGYNY

The conclusion of Joyce's text seems to imply that the artist's notorious misogyny will prove to be still another dimension (and limitation) of his youthful priggishness. The pervasive irony that tinges the hero's scrupulous devotions and gives his aesthetic theory that "true scholastic stink" surely informs his relations with women—from his mother and Dante Riordan to Emma and the unnamed bird-girl he transfigures on the beach. In a tone of gentle mockery, Joyce makes clear to his audience that Stephen's fear of women and his contempt for sensuous life are among the many inhibitions that stifle his creativity. Before he can become a true priest of the eternal imagination, Stephen must first divest himself of "the spiritual-heroic refrigerating apparatus" that characterizes the egocentric aesthete. Narcissism and misogyny are adolescent traits he has to outgrow on the path to artistic maturity. Not until the epic *Ulysses* will a new model begin to emerge, one that recognizes the need for the intellectual artist to make peace with the mother/lover of his dreams and to incorporate into his masterful work those mysterious breaks, flows, gaps, and ruptures associated with the repressed and sublimated flow of male-female desire.

# Stephen's Gradual Disengagement

Arnold Goldman

Arnold Goldman analyzes Stephen's alternating cycles of involvement and disengagement with the world around him. Goldman argues that Stephen's emotional detachment gradually increases to the point that he rejects the offer of the priesthood as a career, and that his flight at the end of the novel is an ambiguous mix of escape and engagement. Arnold Goldman taught English at the Universities of Manchester and Sussex in England and at Smith College in Northampton, Massachusetts. He is the author of *The Joyce Paradox, James Joyce,* and scholarly articles published in the *James Joyce Quarterly* and the *Minnesota Review.*

There is considerable reference to Stephen's growing indifference in the *Portrait.* In human terms, the instances most often reflect forms of self-protection against a hostile environment. They extend over a wide period of time and the analogy between the artist and the indifferent God with which Stephen completes his 'esthetics' is their culmination (or quasi-theological justification). The novel in this respect moves towards an explicit statement of its implicit concerns.

The first hint of detachment is a single short reference. Unjustly pandied at Clongowes,

> Stephen knelt down quickly pressing his beaten hands to his sides. To think of them beaten and swollen with pain all in a moment made him feel so sorry for them as if they were not his own but someone else's that he felt sorry for.

The merest suggestion of a distancing is present here. Stephen's response should be contrasted with the self-pitying reverie of his own death as he lay in the infirmary earlier—'He might die. . . . Wells would be sorry.'

Excerpted from *The Joyce Paradox: Form and Freedom in His Fiction,* by Arnold Goldman. Copyright ©1966 by Arnold Goldman. Reprinted with permission from Northwestern University Press.

## DETACHMENT LEADS TO OBJECTIVITY AND INACTION

Verging on adolescence in Dublin, Stephen

> was angry with himself for being young and the prey of rest-
> less foolish impulses, angry also with the change of fortune
> which was reshaping the world about him into a vision of
> squalor and insincerity. Yet his anger lent nothing to the vi-
> sion. He chronicled with patience what he saw, detaching
> himself from it and testing its mortifying flavour in secret.

As 'chronicled' hints, this detachment is synchronized—
whether as cause or result—to the growth and expression of
his artistic nature. The relation between experience and perception stated here is interesting. Instead of Stephen's 'kinetic' response (his anger) diminishing the value of his perception by introducing an element of bias, it leaves it
unaffected ('lent nothing'). There follow some pages of his
'chronicled' observations, his aunt's kitchen, 'the narrow
breakfast room,' 'a children's party at Harold's Cross,' related
almost inconsequentially, in the manner of the *Epiphanies*.[1]

When Stephen is in this mood, however, the detachment
seems to hinder action. On the tram with Emma, 'he stood
listlessly in his place, seemingly a tranquil watcher of the
scene before him.'

It is through this narrow wedge that the image of the artist
as a renouncer of personal experience enters the novel, in
tacit conflict with Stephen's desire for such experience.
Here, Stephen's unpremeditated, almost undesired, indifferent response to Emma's flirting becomes the apparent pre-
condition for his first poem, already discussed. As the artist,
in such a situation, becomes more self-conscious of what
appears a necessary response in him if he is to turn his experience into art, his problem acquires complexity.

Later, remembering the night he had been attacked by
Belvedere classmates, Stephen

> wondered why he bore no malice now to those who had tor-
> mented him. He had not forgotten a whit of their cowardice
> and cruelty but the memory of it called forth no anger from
> him. All the descriptions of fierce love and hatred which he
> had met in books had seemed to him therefore unreal. Even
> that night as he stumbled homewards along Jones's Road he
> had felt that some power was divesting him of that sudden
> woven anger as easily as a fruit is divested of its soft ripe peel.

1. According to J.S. Atherton, 'Each of the three passages beginning with ["He was sitting"] forms an "epiphany".'

The objects of Stephen's detachment broaden to include his parents and their contemporaries. In a Cork barroom, embarrassedly watching his father drink with cronies, he thinks,

> An abyss of fortune or of temperament sundered him from them. His mind seemed older than theirs: it shone coldly on their strifes and happiness and regrets like a moon upon a younger earth. No life or youth stirred in him as it had stirred in them. . . . Nothing stirred within his soul but a cold and cruel and loveless lust.

As the point of view holds the narrator to the present instant, we can have no comment on the permanence of this mood. How basic it is is for us to decide, and to the extent that we think it is, Stephen is deprived of essential freedom. But the mode of the narrative leaves it equally moot whether Stephen's later panting desire for a wide experience of life means, on the other hand, that he has passed beyond stages of indifference and coldness directed towards that which he feels hostile to him.

## CYCLES OF EXPERIENCE AND WITHDRAWAL

In the present context, Stephen's indifference is brought into contact with the notion of cyclic movement ('vast inhuman cycles of activity'). The connection is soon made even more explicit as Stephen, with a month's initiation into Dublin brothels, sits at his schoolroom desk:

> The equation on the page of his scribbler began to spread out a widening tail, eyed and starred like a peacock's; and, when the eyes and stars of its indices had been eliminated, began slowly to fold itself together again. The indices appearing and disappearing were eyes opening and closing; the eyes opening and closing were stars being born and being quenched. The vast cycle of starry life bore his weary mind outward to its verge and inward to its centre, a distant music accompanying him outward and inward. What music? The music came nearer and he recalled the words, the words of Shelley's fragment upon the moon wandering companionless, pale for weariness. The stars began to crumble and a cloud of fine star-dust fell through space.
> The dull light fell more faintly upon the page whereon another equation began to unfold itself slowly and to spread abroad its widening tail. It was his own soul going forth to experience, unfolding itself sin by sin, spreading abroad the balefire of its burning stars and folding back upon itself, fading slowly, quenching its own lights and fires. They were quenched: and the cold darkness filled chaos.
> A cold lucid indifference reigned in his soul. At his first violent sin he had felt a wave of vitality pass out of him and had

feared to find his body or his soul maimed by the excess. Instead the vital wave had carried him on its bosom out of himself and back again when it receded: and no part of body or soul had been maimed, but a dark peace had been established between them. The chaos in which his ardour extinguished itself was a cold indifferent knowledge of himself.

The 'soul going forth to experience' also 'fold[s] back upon itself, fading slowly, quenching its own lights and fires'. The form of movement embodied in the various metaphors is a diastolic-systolic cycle.[2] This too has its antecedents in the novel: the 'roar like a train at night' made by closing and opening the flaps of the ears in the Clongowes refectory, later explicitly connected with the rhythm of school life—term, vacation, term, vacation, etc.; the reading down and then up of the geography flyleaf inscription (Stephen Dedalus/Class of Elements/Clongowes Wood College/etc.); the celebration of Stephen's protest to Conmee among a shower of thrown caps by a circle of boys who 'closed round [Stephen] in a ring' and then 'broke away in all directions', leaving him 'alone . . . happy and free.'

The movements implied in Stephen's meditation on the scribbler suggest his developing formulation of his relation to his experience. It appears as a process of alternate entrance into and immediate disengagement from experience, paralleled psychologically in the movements of desire and indifference, attraction and repulsion, longing and fear. Stephen's attention moves in and out, centripetally and centrifugally, in towards himself and out towards the universe.

## THE ALTERNATING PATTERN GAINS FORCE AND SIGNIFICANCE

The alternations increase in force and significance—the pattern of resonance—as the novel proceeds. Rejection of the Church and acceptance of the artist's calling comprise the final major oscillation in the novel's structure—though the contrary modes are by then so implanted as to hover about the remainder in implication, as has been seen in the case of the 'esthetics' and as will be discussed apropos of Stephen's diary. The structural utility of an increase in force in each episode accounts for two alterations which [critic] Kevin Sullivan has noted Joyce made when refashioning the events of his own life into the novel: that 'Joyce's refusal of a vocation

2. a 'Kinetic' cycle essentially dissimilar to 'that cardiac condition which the Italian physiologist Luigi Galvani . . . called the enchantment of the heart'

is quite distinct from his later rejection of Catholicism'—in the *Portrait* they are conflated—and that 'Joyce thought longer and more seriously about becoming a Jesuit' than does Stephen, whose rejection of the order is immediately consequent upon his 'temptation.'

By not carrying the different possibilities of a career in the Church and a calling in Art along together, Joyce relinquishes the opportunity to present Stephen's choice as between alternatives equally distinct. The *meaning* of the priesthood to Stephen is concrete enough—'He longed for the minor sacred offices, to be vested with the tunicle of the subdeacon at high mass'—for however much he romanticizes the 'voice bidding him approach, offering him secret knowledge and secret power' he knows the very feel of the life—'The trembling odour of the long corridors of Clongowes came back to him and he heard the discreet murmour of the burning gas flames.' What he is rejecting this *for* cannot be so precisely rendered. It is 'some instinct' which turns him against acceptance, but the burden of detail is on what is being rejected— 'the raw reddish glow . . . on the shaven gills of the priests.' The narrative moves on negative wheels: 'He would never swing the thurible before the tabernacle as priest.'

The irony of the situation, and Stephen recognizes it, is that the disengagement precedes any definite engagement. The alternative to the Order is 'disorder':

> He smiled to think that it was this disorder, the misrule and confusion of his father's house and the stagnation of vegetable life, which was to win the day in his soul.

The point is brought home a moment later:

> He pushed open the latchless door of the porch and passed through the naked hallway into the kitchen. A group of his brothers and sisters was sitting round the table. Tea was nearly over and only the last of the second watered tea remained in the bottom of the small glass jars and jampots which did service for teacups. Discarded crusts and lumps of sugared bread, turned brown by the tea which had been poured over them, lay scattered on the table. Little wells of tea lay here and there on the board and a knife with a broken ivory handle was stuck through the pith of a ravaged turnover.

The 'remorse' which Stephen feels at the sight of this is the emotion by which Ireland—home, fatherland and Church— attempts to keep her own. It is clear to Stephen that if he would go into orders he could rescue his family from this squalor. It was for that, he has been told, he has been educated: 'All that had been denied them had been freely given to him, the eldest.'. . .

## THE FINAL ENGAGEMENT IS AMBIGUOUS

Towards the end of this chapter Stephen is vouchsafed the vision of the wading girl, who appears as if in reply to his ecstatic choice of vocation:

> This was the call of life to his soul not the dull gross voice of the world of duties and despair, not the inhuman voice that had called him to the pale service of the altar. An instant of wild flight had delivered him. . . .
>
> His soul had arisen from the grave of boyhood, spurning her graveclothes. Yes! Yes! Yes! He would create proudly out of the freedom and power of his soul, as the great artificer whose name he bore, a living thing, new and soaring and beautiful, impalpable, imperishable.

But if 'no word [broke] the holy silence of his ecstasy' in her presence, one has but to turn the page to realize that there is still an area of life to which Stephen is attached, as artist and man:

> He drained his third cup of watery tea to the dregs and set to chewing the crusts of fried bread that were scattered near him, staring into the dark pool of the jar . . . . The box of pawn tickets at his elbow had just been rifled . . . .
>
> —Is your lazy bitch of a brother gone out yet?

That Stephen's latterly presented 'engagement' is merely a flourish imperfectly grafted upon a basically cold and retiring nature is at the root of much uneasiness over Stephen, even among his admirers. To his detractors, the engagement is a 'set-up': [critic Hugh Kenner says]

> the exalted instant, emerging at the end of the book, of freedom, of vocation, of Stephen's destiny, winging his way above the waters at the side of the hawk-like man: the instant of promise on which the crushing ironies of *Ulysses* are to fall.

[Critic] Richard Ellmann goes half the distance here with Hugh Kenner, agreeing that the flight at the *Portrait*'s end is based on an illusory notion, but claiming that the fallen state pictured in *Ulysses* contains a saving grace:

> Flying for Stephen turns out to be paradoxically a lapse from humanity, a failure; while falling is a recognition of life's saving lowliness, a success. . . . Through flying beyond life we learn only our own presumption; through falling into life, even into low life, we educate ourselves into community with others.

Rarely does a critic hold out against seeing the ending as

unironical. [Critic] Eugene Waith, writing against the views of Kenner and Caroline Gordon, claims they emphasize 'the theme of the fall while neglecting the theme of creativity.' Waith attempts to relate the two so that 'the fall is assimilated into the preparations for the flight. . . . The flight of Daedalus is not only an escape but a widening of consciousness, an investigation of the unknown.' That what we comprehend under the 'themes' of flight and fall may enter into other relationships Waith does not consider. It is, however, equally likely that fall and flight both increase in scope as the novel proceeds and yet can be regarded as undermining each other.

# CHAPTER 4

# Joyce's Literary Techniques and Devices in *A Portrait*

# Joyce's Epiphanies

Dorothy Van Ghent

Dorothy Van Ghent defines epiphany, the literary term James Joyce introduced to identify the experience of opposing elements or forces coming together and leading to awareness. Van Ghent illustrates her definition with examples of major and minor epiphanies. Moreover, she explains how Stephen's walking moves him toward small and large epiphanies and identifies Stephen's ultimate epiphany as a search for unity, harmony, and meaning. Dorothy Van Ghent taught English at the University of Vermont. She is the author of *The Essential Prose, Willa Cather,* and *Keats: The Myth of the Hero.*

Those moments in the dialectical process[1] when a synthesis is achieved, when certain phrases or sensations or complex experiences suddenly cohere in a larger whole and a meaning shines forth from the whole, Joyce—who introduced the word into literary currency—called "epiphanies." They are "showings-forth" of the nature of reality as the boy is prepared to grasp it. Minor epiphanies mark all the stages of Stephen's understanding, as when the feel of Eileen's hand shows him what Tower of Ivory means, or as when the word "Foetus,"[2] carved on a school desk, suddenly focuses for him in brute clarity his "monstrous way of life." Major epiphanies, occurring at the end of each chapter, mark the chief revelations of the nature of his environment and of his destiny in it. The epiphany is an image, sensuously apprehended and emotionally vibrant, which communicates instantaneously the meaning of experience. It may contain a revelation of a person's character, brief and fleeting, occurring by virtue of some physical trait in the person, as the way big Corrigan looked in the bath:

1. the process of resolving the contradiction between two conflicting forces 2. or fetus, meaning in Latin pregnant

Excerpted from *The English Novel: Form and Function,* by Dorothy Van Ghent (New York: Harper & Row, 1953). Copyright ©1953 by Dorothy Van Ghent, renewed 1981 by Roger Van Ghent. Reprinted with permission from Holt, Rinehart, and Winston.

> He had skin the same colour as the turf-coloured bogwater in the shallow end of the bath and when he walked along the side his feet slapped loudly on the wet tiles and at every step his thighs shook a little because he was fat.

In this kind of use, as revelation through one or two physical traits of the whole mass-formation of a personality, the epiphany is almost precisely duplicable in [Charles] Dickens, as in the spectacle of Miss Havisham leaning on her crutch beside the rotten bridecake, or of Jaggers flourishing his white handkerchief and biting his great forefinger. The minor personalities in the *Portrait* are reduced to something very like a Dickensian "signature"—as Heron with his bird-beaked face and bird-name, Davin with his peasant turns of speech, Lynch whose "long slender flattened skull beneath the long pointed cap brought before Stephen's mind the image of a hooded reptile." Or the epiphany may be a kind of "still life" with which are associated deep and complex layers of experience and emotion. In the following passage, for instance, the sordor of Stephen's home, the apprehensive and guilty image of the bath at Clongowes, and the bestiality he associates with the bogholes of Ireland, are illuminated simultaneously by a jar of drippings on the table.

> He drained his third cup of watery tea to the dregs and set to chewing the crusts of fried bread that were scattered near him, staring into the dark pool of the jar. The yellow dripping had been scooped out like a boghole, and the pool under it brought back to his memory the dark turfcoloured water of the bath at Clongowes.

Here the whole complex of home, school, and nation is epitomized in one object and shot through with the emotion of rejection. The epiphany is usually the result of a gradual development of the emotional content of associations, as they accrete with others. Among Stephen's childish impressions is that of "a woman standing at the halfdoor of a cottage with a child in her arms," and

> it would be lovely to sleep for one night in that cottage before the fire of smoking turf, in the dark lit by the fire, in the warm dark, breathing the smell of the peasants, air and rain and turf and corduroy . . .

The early impression enters into emotional context, later, with the story Davin tells him about stopping at night at the cottage of a peasant woman, and Stephen's image of the woman is for him an epiphany of the soul of Ireland: "a bat-like soul waking to the consciousness of itself in darkness

and secrecy and loneliness." The epiphany is dynamic, acti-
vated by the form-seeking urgency in experience, and itself
feeding later revelations. At the point of exile, Stephen feels,
"under the deepened dusk,"

> the thoughts and desires of the race to which he belonged flit-
> ting like bats, across the dark country lanes, under trees by
> the edges of streams and near the pool mottled bogs.

## MAJOR EPIPHANIES CORRESPOND
## WITH CLIMAXES IN EACH CHAPTER

The major epiphanies in the book occur as the symbolic cli-
maxes of the larger dialectical movements constituting each
of the five chapters. As [critic] Hugh Kenner has pointed out,
in his essay "*The Portrait* in Perspective," each of the chapters begins with a multitude of warring impressions, and
each develops toward an emotionally apprehended unity;
each succeeding chapter liquidates the previous synthesis
and subjects its elements to more adult scrutiny in a constantly enlarging field of perception, and develops toward its
own synthesis and affirmation. In each chapter, out of the
multitude of elements with which it opens, some one chief
conflict slowly shapes itself. In the first, among all the be-
wildering impressions that the child's mind entertains, the
deeper conflict is that between his implicit trust in the authority of his elders—his Jesuit teachers, the older boys in
the school, his father and Mr. Casey and Dante—and his actual sense of insecurity. His elders, since they apparently
know the meaning of things, must therefore incarnate perfect justice and moral and intellectual consistency. But the
child's real experience is of mad quarrels at home over Parnell and the priests, and at school the frivolous cruelty of the
boys, the moral chaos suggested by the smugging in the
square and the talk about stealing the altar wine, and the
sadism of Father Dolan with his pandybat. With Stephen's
visit to the rector at the end of the chapter, the conflict is resolved. Justice is triumphant—even a small boy with weak
eyes can find it; he is greeted like a hero on his emergence
from the rector's office; his consolidation with his human
environment is gloriously affirmed.

The second chapter moves straight from that achievement
of emotional unity into other baffling complexities, coinci-
dent with the family's removal to Dublin. The home life is increasingly squalid, the boy more lonely and restless. In Si-

mon Dedalus' account of his conversation with the rector of Clongowes about the incident of the pandying, what had seemed, earlier, to be a triumph of justice and an affirmation of intelligent moral authority by Stephen's elders is revealed as cruel, stupid indifference. In the episode in which Stephen is beaten for "heresy," the immediate community of his schoolfellows shows itself as false, shot through with stupidity and sadism. More importantly, the image of the father is corroded. On the visit to Cork, Simon appears to the boy's despairing judgment as besotted, self-deluded, irresponsible—and with the corruption of the father-image his whole picture of society suffers the same ugly damage. On the same visit, Stephen's early dim apprehension of sin and guilt is raised into horrible prominence by the word "Foetus" which he sees inscribed on the desk at Queen's College and which symbolizes for him all his adolescent monstrosity (the more monstrous in that Simon looks with obscene sentimentality on the desk carvings, thus condemning the whole world for Stephen in his own sickened sense of guilt). Meanwhile, his idealistic longings for beauty and purity and gentleness and certitude have concentrated in a vaguely erotic fantasy of the dream-girl Mercedes in her rose-cottage. Again, at the end of the chapter, Stephen's inner conflict is resolved in an emotional unity, a new vision of the relationships between the elements of experience. The synthesis is constituted here by a triumphant integration of the dream of Mercedes with the encounter with the whore. It is "sin" that triumphs, but sublimated as an ideal unity, pure and gentle and beautiful and emotionally securing.

## THE SIGNIFICANCE OF STEPHEN'S WALKING

As Hugh Kenner has observed, in the essay cited above, the predominant physical activity in *The Portrait* that accompanies Stephen's mental dialectics, as he moves through analysis to new provisional syntheses, is the activity of walking; his ambulatory movements take him into new localities, among new impressions, as his mind moves correspondingly into new spiritual localities that subsume the older ones and readjust them as parts of a larger whole. Living in Dublin, his walks take him toward the river and the sea—toward the fluid thing that, like the "stream" of his thoughts, seems by its searching mobility to imply a more engrossing reality. At first, in Dublin, the boy

contented himself with circling timidly round the neighbour-
ing square or, at most, going half way down one of the side
streets; but when he had made a skeleton map of the city in
his mind he followed boldly one of its central lines until he
reached the Custom House. . . . The vastness and strangeness
of the life suggested to him by the bales of merchandise
stocked along the walls or swung aloft out of the holds of
steamers wakened again in him the unrest which had sent
him wandering in the evening from garden to garden in
search of Mercedes. . . . A vague dissatisfaction grew up within
him as he looked on the quays and on the river and on the
lowering skies and yet he continued to wander up and down
day after day as if he really sought someone that eluded him.

On his visit to Cork with his father, in his wanderings in the
brothel section of Dublin, on his seaward walk at the end of
the fourth chapter when his chief revelation of personal destiny comes to him, on his later walks between home and the
university, on his walk with Lynch during which he recapit-
ulates his aesthetics, and with Cranly when he formulates
his decision not "to serve"—on each of these peripatetic ex-
cursions, his mind moves toward more valid organizations
of experience, as his feet carry him among other voices and
images and into more complex fields of perception.

In the third chapter of the book, the hortations[3] to which
he is exposed during the retreat pull him down from his exaltation in sin and analyze his spiritual state into a multitude
of subjective horrors that threaten to engulf him entirely and
jeopardize his immortal soul. The conflict is resolved during
a long walk which he takes blindly and alone, and that carries him to a strange place where he feels able to make his
confession. A new synthesis is achieved through his participation in the Mass. Chapter 4 shows him absorbed in a
dream of a saintly career, but his previous emotional affir
mation has been frittered and wasted away in the perfor-
mance of pedantically formal acts of piety, and he is afflicted
with doubts, insecurities, rebellions. Release from conflict
comes with a clear refusal of a vocation in the church, ob-
jectified by his decision to enter the university. And again it
is on a walk that he realizes the measure of the new reality
and the new destiny.

He has abandoned his father to a public house and has set
off toward the river and the sea.

The university! So he had passed beyond the challenge of the

3. strong urgings

sentries who had stood as guardians of his boyhood and had
sought to keep him among them that he might be subject to
them and serve their ends. Pride after satisfaction uplifted
him like long slow waves. The end he had been born to serve
yet did not see had led him to escape by an unseen path: and
now it beckoned to him once more and a new adventure was
about to be opened to him. It seemed to him that he heard
notes of fitful music leaping upwards a tone and downwards
a diminishing fourth, upwards a tone and downwards a major third, like triple-branching flames leaping fitfully, flame
after flame, out of a midnight wood. It was an elfin prelude,
endless and formless; and, as it grew wilder and faster, the
flames leaping out of time, he seemed to hear from under the
boughs and grasses wild creatures racing, their feet pattering
like rain upon the leaves. Their feet passed in pattering tu-
mult over his mind, the feet of hares and rabbits, the feet of
harts and hinds and antelopes, until he heard them no more
and remembered only a proud cadence from Newman:—

—Whose feet are as the feet of harts and underneath the
everlasting arms.

The imagery is that of mobile, going things, increasingly pas-
sionate and swift—first slow waves, then fitful music leaping, then flames, then racing creatures. A phrase of his own
making comes to his lips: "A day of dappled seaborne
clouds." The dappled color and the sea movement of the
clouds are of the same emotional birth as the images of music and flames. All are of variety and mobility of perception,
as against stasis and restriction. Physically Stephen is escaping from his father—and the public house where he has left
Simon is the sordid core of that Dublin environment whose
false claims on his allegiance he is trying to shake off; at the
same time he is realizing a "first noiseless sundering" with
his mother, a break that is related to his decision against ac-
cepting a vocation in the church. Dublin, the tangible and vo-
cal essence of his nationality, and the Roman church, the
mold of his adolescent intellect, have failed to provide him
with a vision of reality corresponding with his experience,
and he thinks in terms of a movement beyond these—toward
another and mysterious possible synthesis. "And underneath
the everlasting arms": the phrase from Newman implies an
ultimate unity wherein all the real is held in wholeness. Toward this problematic divine embrace Stephen moves, but it
is only problematic and he can approach it only by his own
movement. The epiphany which confronts him in this moment on the beach is a manifestation of his destiny in terms
of a winged movement. He hears his name, Dedalus, called

out, and the name seems to be prophetic.

> . . . at the name of the fabulous artificer, he seemed to hear the noise of dim waves and to see a winged form flying above the waves and slowly climbing the air . . . a hawklike man flying sunward above the sea, a prophecy of the end he had been born to serve and had been following through the mists of childhood and boyhood, a symbol of the artist forging anew in his workshop out of the sluggish matter of the earth a new soaring impalpable imperishable being . . .

The ending of Chapter 4 presents this new consciousness in terms of an ecstatic state of sensibility. It is marked by the radiant image of the girl standing in a rivulet of tide, seeming "like one whom magic had changed into the likeness of a strange and beautiful seabird . . . touched with the wonder of mortal beauty," while his own life cries wildly to him, "To live, to err, to fall, to triumph, to recreate life out of life!" The girl is a "wild angel" that has appeared to him, to "throw open before him in an instant of ecstasy the ways of error and glory." The batlike woman-soul of his race, flitting in darkness and secrecy and loneliness, has given place to this angelic emissary from "the fair courts of life," of strange seabird beauty, inviting him to exile across waters and into other languages, as the sun-assailing and perhaps doomed Icarus. And it is in the flights of birds that Stephen, standing on the steps of the university library, in the last chapter, reads like an ancient haruspex[4] the sanction of his exile.

## STEPHEN'S SEARCH FOR UNITY, HARMONY AND MEANING

With Chapter 5, Stephen's new consciousness of destiny is subjected to intellectual analysis. Here, during his long walks with Lynch and Cranly, all the major elements that have exerted emotional claims upon him—his family, church, nation, language—are scrutinized dryly, their claims torn down and scattered in the youthfully pedantic and cruel light of the adolescent's proud commitment to art. Here also he formulates his aesthetics, the synthesis which he has contrived out of a few scraps of medieval learning. In his aesthetic formulation, the names he borrows from [theologian and philosopher Thomas] Aquinas for "the three things needed for beauty"—*integritas, consonantia, claritas*—are names for those aspects of reality—wholeness, harmoniousness, signif-

---

4. a priest in ancient Rome who practiced divination by the inspection of the entrails of animals

icant character—that he has been seeking all his life, from earliest childhood. His aesthetic formulation is thus a synthesis of the motivations of his psychological life from the beginning; and the vocation of artist which he has chosen is the vocation of one who consciously sets himself the task of apprehending and then representing in his art whatever wholeness, harmony, and meaning the world has.

In an earlier version of *The Portrait,* called *Stephen Hero,* it is said that the task of the artist is to

> disentangle the subtle soul of the image from its mesh of defining circumstances most exactly and "re-embody" it in artistic circumstances chosen as the most exact for it in its new office . . .

The "new office" of the image is to communicate to others the significant character of a complete and harmonious body of experience. The artist is a midwife of epiphanies. Joyce's doctrine of the epiphany assumes that reality does have wholeness and harmony—even as Stephen as a child premises these, and with the same trustfulness—and that it will radiantly show forth its character and its meaning to the prepared consciousness, for it is only in the body of reality that meaning can occur and only there that the artist can find it. This is essentially a religious interpretation of the nature of reality and of the artist's function. It insists on the objectivity of the wholeness, harmony, and meaning, and on the objectivity of the revelation—the divine showing-forth.

At Clongowes Wood, there had been a picture of the earth on the first page of Stephen's geography, "a big ball in the middle of clouds," and on the flyleaf of the book Stephen had written his name and "where he was."

> Stephen Dedalus
> Class of Elements
> Clongowes Wood College
> Sallins
> County Kildare
> Ireland
> Europe
> The World
> The Universe

His ambulatory, dialectical journey is a quest to find the defining unity, the composing harmony, and the significant character of each of these broadening localities containing Stephen Dedalus, and the intelligible relationships making each functional in the next. It is an attempt, by progressive stages, at last to bring the term "Stephen Dedalus" into relationship with the term "The Universe." Through the book he moves from one geographical and spiritual orbit to another, "walking" in lengthening radius until he is ready to take up flight. As a child at Clongowes it had pained him that he did not know what came after the universe.

> What was after the universe? Nothing. But was there anything round the universe to show where it stopped before the nothing place began? It could not be a wall but there could be a thin thin line there all round everything. It was very big to think about everything and everywhere. Only God could do that. He tried to think what a big thought that must be but he could think only of God. God was God's name just as his name was Stephen. *Dieu* was the French for God and that was God's name too; and when anyone prayed to God and said Dieu then God knew at once that was a French person that was praying. But though there were different names for God in all the different languages in the world and God understood what all the people who prayed said in their different languages still God remained always the same God and God's real name was God.

At the end of the book Stephen is prepared at least to set forth on the "dappled, seaborne clouds" that float beyond Ireland and over Europe. His search is still to find out "what came after the universe." The ultimate epiphany is withheld, the epiphany of "everything and everywhere" as one and harmonious and meaningful. But it is prophesied in "God's real name," as Stephen's personal destiny is prophesied in his own name "Dedalus." It is to be found in the labyrinth of language that contains all human revelation vouchsafed by divine economy, and to be found by the artist in naming the names.

# The Epiphany That Reveals Stephen's Fate

Edmund L. Epstein

Edmund L. Epstein analyzes the five episodes of the epiphany in chapter 4 when Stephen feels his fate— his vocation—is revealed. In the introduction and episodes 1 and 2, Stephen severs ties with parents and authority figures and recognizes clearly the vocation he has rejected. After a look back at hazy Dublin, Stephen sees a clear image of his Irish race in the third episode. In the fourth episode his vocation is evoked in the vision of the bird-girl, and in the fifth a vision of fulfillment is symbolized by the rose. In the coda he awakens from his dream as the tide rises. Edmund L. Epstein taught English at Queens College of the City University of New York. He has edited the journals *James Joyce Review* and *Language and Style* and the book *A Starchamber Quiry: A Joyce Centennial Publication.*

The third section of chapter 4 is extremely complex, both in its form and in its symbolism. All of the episodes in *A Portrait* are carefully chosen for their symbolic importance in the life of the developing artist, but this section contains the moment when the artist, like Hamlet, feels his fate cry out, when the vocation he has been pursuing both consciously and unconsciously becomes manifest to him, when "the end he had been born to serve yet did not see" finally blazes before him.

This section is built in five parts, with an introduction and a coda. Each of these five parts, with the exception of the second, contains a moment of exaltation in which one aspect of Stephen's vocation becomes clear to him.

Excerpted from *The Ordeal of Stephen Dedalus: The Conflict of the Generations in James Joyce's* A Portrait of the Artist as a Young Man, by Edmund L. Epstein. Copyright ©1971 by Southern Illinois University Press. Reprinted by permission of the publisher.

## INTRODUCTION

Almost every word in the introduction is significant. "He could wait no longer;" it is his father for whom he could wait no longer, and once he strides off toward his vocation he dreads being called back: "He set off abruptly for the Bull, walking rapidly lest his father's shrill whistle might call him back." He rounds the curve at the police barracks—another symbol of paternal control—and is "safe" from his father's pursuit, a significant choice of words. (All the unconscious symbolism in the book comes to the surface in this section.)

It is at this point that he experiences another sundering of old ties—he separates his life from his mother's. She had attempted to bind him to the past; with an almost reflex action he throws off the thought of her. His powers of "darkness" help him: "A dim antagonism gathered force within him and darkened his mind as a cloud against her disloyalty." So he has cast off both his parents.

## FIRST EPISODE

The thought of the university sets off the first episode of exaltation. For the first time the whole trend of his past life is completely clear to him.

> The university! So he had passed beyond the challenge of the sentries who had stood as guardians of his boyhood and had sought to keep him among them that he might be subject to them and serve their ends. Pride after satisfaction uplifted him like long slow waves. The end he had been born to serve yet did not see had led him to escape by an unseen path.

This realization of his escape from the nets of the past, from his actual parents and from all the other fathers of his environment, sets off the flames and darkness of his introduction to sex and of his vocation.

> It seemed to him that he heard notes of fitful music leaping upwards a tone and downwards a diminished fourth, upwards a tone and downwards a major third, like triple-branching flames leaping fitfully, flame after flame, out of a midnight wood. It was an elfin prelude, endless and formless; and, as it grew wilder and faster, the flames leaping out of time, he seemed to hear from under the boughs and grasses wild creatures racing, their feet pattering like rain upon the leaves.

The "formlessness" of his prelude and the sounds of living, moving nature are reminiscent of other aspects of his vocation—his acceptance of the facts of the "funnaminal world,"

(*FW* [1] 244.13) the universe of random chances, the "collide-orescape" (*FW* 143.28) which is his to reproduce and mold.

## SECOND EPISODE

The second episode contains no exaltation, merely conscious rejection by Stephen of alternatives to his vocation. Stephen asks himself why he has turned aside from what he had "so often thought to be his destiny . . . He had refused. Why?" His question is answered by the appearance of the cloddish Christian Brothers "stained yellow or red or livid by the sea," the "cold mad feary father" (*FW* 628.2), "Old Father Ocean" (*U* 50), whose "infrahuman odour" he dreads. Like Stephen's school friends later on, the Christian Brothers have surrendered to the father. "Brothers" not fathers, they have been "stained" by the paternal sea; they are the possession of the father now and are incapable of independent action. They move as a unit; like the figures in Stephen's dream recorded in his diary "one does not seem to stand quite apart from another." They are selfless and serviceable; Stephen is independent, self-conscious, serving nothing but his own vocation. . . .

Stephen then questions the source of his love of words. His self-examination is completely appropriate in this context—words are the tools of his vocation. He never answers his own question, whether it is the rhythms of words he enjoys more than the "inner world of individual emotions" which he will convey in "a lucid supple periodic prose." At any rate, it is not the raw matter of the world which is primary in his art but his vision of it, his transmutation of it into art. He is not the servant of the world, but the conscious master of it. . . .

The last part of the second episode prepares the way for the ceremony of vocation. Stephen contemplates Dublin through the haze. The modern city lies before him, but his thoughts pierce through; as we later discover, "the ghost of the ancient kingdom of the Danes had looked forth through the vesture of the hazewrapped city.". . .

Equally important in this context is that the revelation to Stephen is of the past of his race, the Irish. The past of his race provides the greater part of the material of his major work. More to the immediate point, however, his vision provides Stephen with his goal in *A Portrait*—to recreate the conscience of his race, the past of which begins to be clear

1. *FW* is *Finnegans Wake*; *U* is *Ulysses*; all other quotations come from *A Portrait*.

to him at this point. It is this concept of "race" which sets off the third episode, the second wave of exaltation that sweeps over him, the real beginning of his ceremony of ordination.

## THIRD EPISODE

The beginning of the second wave of exaltation is disheartenment: "Disheartened [by his vision of the Irish race's subjection], he raised his eyes toward the slowdrifting clouds, dappled and seaborne." The reminder of his tools as an artist, the supple periodic prose that he is to mold to tell the story of his race, lifts his depression and sets off a quiet wave of exaltation, in which ancestral voices seem to announce his coming:

> The Europe they [the clouds] had come from lay out there beyond the Irish Sea, Europe of strange tongues and valleyed and woodbegirt and citadelled and of entrenched and marshalled races. He heard a confused music within him as of memories and names which he was almost conscious of but could not capture even for an instant.

Both Stephen and Joyce really believed in the existences of national races; neither of them was a modern internationalist. Joyce was an old-fashioned nationalist, of the school of [German philosopher and critic Johann] Herder and [British essayist and poet] Matthew Arnold and [Italian patriot] Mazzini. Stephen contemptuously rejects MacCann's internationalism later on in *A Portrait*, and in *Ulysses* he pours scorn on international arbitration arranged by peaceloving monarchs. If the Irish race did not exist it would be useless to try to "forge in the smithy of [his] soul" its uncreated conscience. . . .

The mention of "race" with all of its mystical and Mazzinian overtones, sets off the process of ordination. Stephen hears a "voice from beyond the world." The voice is, on the literal level, the voice of his friends, calling to him jocularly as they fall into the water, but in Stephen's state of heightened awareness, they are the voices of his race hailing him *vates,* the crowned poet. *"Stephanos,* my crown" Stephen thinks in *Ulysses* (*U* 210); here "Stephanos!" is shouted by his friends. "The Dedalus" combines the Celtic way of referring to a chief of a clan with Stephen's "strange name"; to Stephen it seems that they are acknowledging "his mild proud sovereignty." They are all "absorbed" sons. Joyce leaves no room for doubt that they are entirely the property of the cold father; like the livid, yellow and red Christian Brothers they are "corpsewhite," "pallid golden," "rawly tanned," and they are covered with cold sea-water.

> The roughhewn stones of the sloping breakwater over which they scrambled in their horseplay . . . gleamed with cold wet lustre. The towels with which they smacked their bodies were heavy with cold seawater: and drenched with cold brine was their matted hair.

They dive, or fall, back into the cold, infrahuman sea, shouting out, like Icarus, "O, cripes, I'm drownded!" They are symbolically the "belated" race of the Irish that Stephen will arouse. Meanwhile they are completely in the power of the father. At the mention of his name, the name he had once defended from Father Dolan, that of the "fabulous artificer," "he seemed to hear the noise of dim waves and to see a winged form flying above the waves and slowly climbing the air." He knows himself perfectly at that "timeless" moment:

> What did it mean? Was it a quaint device opening a page of some medieval book of prophecies and symbols, a hawklike man flying sunward above the sea, a prophecy of the end he had been born to serve and had been following through the mists of childhood and boyhood, a symbol of the artist forging anew in his workshop out of the sluggish matter of the earth a new soaring impalpable imperishable being?

Stephen feels as if he is flying: "the body he knew was purified in a breath and delivered of incertitude and made radiant and commingled with the element of the spirit.". . .

The third episode ends with another realization by Stephen of the "pale service" he has escaped. He starts up nervously to stride onward, accompanied by the flames and darkness of his vocation, and with creation singing in his throat.

> He could no longer quench the flame in his blood. He felt his cheeks aflame and his throat throbbing with song. There was a lust of wandering in his feet that burned to set out for the ends of the earth. On! On! his heart seemed to cry. Evening would deepen above the sea, night fall upon the plains, dawn glimmer before the wanderer and show him strange fields and hills and faces. . . . Already one long oval bank of sand lay warm and dry amid the wavelets. Here and there warm isles of sand gleamed above the shallow tide . . . The water of the rivulet was dark with endless drift and mirrored the high-drifting clouds. . . . the grey warm air was still.

He looks toward Howth,[2] which is to become the supreme father symbol in *Finnegans Wake,* and picks up a stick, the ancestor of his ashplant, his "augur's rod," in *Ulysses,* the

---

2. a peninsula several miles northeast of Dublin, the site of Howth Castle and of the high hill of Howth

other half of his costume as a *vates,* the companion symbol to his crown, the hat. Thus equipped, he is ready for the next stage of his ordination.

### FOURTH EPISODE

The fourth episode contains the highest and most powerful exaltation, that evoked by the birdlike girl on the beach. Now the water of the rivulet is "dark with drift," and he and the girl are "alone." He is "alone" and she is "alone and still;" it is at this point that Stephen's prediction, made as a very young boy, comes true.

> [Stephen and the "unsubstantial image which his soul constantly beheld"] would be alone, surrounded by darkness and silence: and in that moment of supreme tenderness he would be transfigured.

In this intensely self-revelatory episode the symbolic meaning of the girl is perfectly clear to Stephen.

> A wild angel had appeared to him, the angel of mortal youth and beauty, an envoy from the fair courts of life, to throw open before him in an instant of ecstasy the gates of all the ways of error and glory. . . . He felt . . . the earth beneath him, the earth that had borne him, had taken him to her breast.

The girl symbolizes the realm of "error," "lots," chances, that he has chosen over the dead certainties of the altar of the "absorbing" father; she is the earth itself, the "vegetable chaos" of earthly life. The girl on the beach is the symbolic descendant of Eileen Vance whom Stephen was going to marry, as a baby, thus arousing the frightened, jealous fury of the father; she is E.C., the girl who lingered on the tram step for Stephen's word of love, which did not come. She is Mercedes and the Virgin to whom he prayed in his fear during the sermons on hell. She is the prostitute who initiated him into sex amid flickering gasflames. (In the 1904 essay "Portrait" the phrase here applied to the bird-girl—an "angel of mortal youth and beauty, an envoy from the fair courts of life" describes the prostitute.) Later she will be the temptress of his villanelle and Molly Bloom [in *Ulysses*] and, perhaps, both Anna Livia and Issy in *Finnegans Wake.* Basically, however, she is the dark, warm Earth.

The exclamation of Stephen's soul, "Heavenly God!" accompanying an "outburst of profane joy," is not inconsistent. The sacred and profane here join. Matter and spirit unite in a mystical marriage which, like the archetypal marriages in

*Finnegans Wake*, is incestuous, the son married with Mother Earth or, as in the later chapters of the *Wake*, with his sister, like "boyrun to sibster" (*FW* 465.17)

## FIFTH EPISODE

The fifth episode is the most mysterious of all. After his powerful "flight" in the fourth episode, Stephen sinks down "that the peace and silence of the evening might still the riot of his blood." He feels the earth beneath him and the heavens above him. "He closed his eyes in the languor of sleep." He dreams of a vast red rose, "trembling and unfolding, a breaking light, an opening flower." The juxtaposition of Stephen's mystical understanding of the heavens and the earth and the unfolding, developing red rose of "vegetable life" suggests to me that the red rose is the symbol for Stephen of the universe developing through time to its fulfillment, its *telos*,[3] just as his soul had developed, past obstacles and traps, to its fulfillment in this chapter of ceremonies; Stephen's white rose of innocence has become the red rose of experience, the "rosa mystica" of the litany, with the mystical ceremony of the marriage of earth and heaven. . . .

Stephen's image of the universe as a red flower combines powerful elements of creation and of sexual attack and surrender, and is the symbol of the subject matter of the matured artist which he is going to shape into a new reality.

## CODA

The third part of chapter 4 ends with a coda.[4] Stephen wakes from his dream of the ardent flowers and looks about him. The moon had risen, and the tide was coming in. The last words of the chapter are a version of one of the few phrases from the first sketch of *A Portrait* composed on January 7, 1904, "the few last figures islanded in distant pools," that survived to the final version of *A Portrait:* "The tide was flowing in fast to the land with a low whisper of her waves, islanding a few last figures in distant pools." This survival suggests to me that the section of *A Portrait* containing the "ordination ceremony" is one of the most important in the book, one to which Joyce was leading for many chapters, and one which had been maturing in his mind for ten years.

---

3. in Greek "end"   4. a passage at the end of a musical composition that brings it to a formal close

Indeed, many important things have been achieved in this chapter. The artist's soul has been laid out before us—his love of words, his affinity for warmth and darkness, his quarrel with the signs of the father, coldness and whiteness, his attitude toward absorption by his environment and toward his compatriots and contemporaries who were so absorbed, his acceptance of the "vegetable" realm of development and error and incertitude, and his conscious acceptance of maturity, sexual and emotional, as an indispensable sign of his vocation. He has also acquired his crown, *stephanos,* the symbol of creative mastery as well as a reminder of his important name. He has acquired his stick, his sword "Nothung," his "augur's rod," his "lifewand," (as it becomes in *Finnegans Wake*) the symbol of his mastery over the past of his "race," over the "dead" whom he is to awaken.

# The Motif as a Device

Marvin Magalaner and Richard M. Kain

Marvin Magalaner and Richard M. Kain explain how Joyce's use of the motif unifies and strengthens the novel. The authors trace the single motif of Stephen's guilt and ridicule or punishment through several episodes in the first two chapters. Marvin Magalaner taught at City College, City University of New York, and lectured at Columbia University and the University of Paris. He is the author of *A Joyce Miscellany* and *A Reader's Guide to the Twentieth-Century English Novel* and editor of *Critical Reviews of "A Portrait of the Artist as a Young Man."* Richard M. Kain, who taught English at the University of Louisville in Kentucky, is the author of *Fabulous Voyager*, a study of *Ulysses,* and *Dublin in the Age of W.B. Yeats and James Joyce.*

The realist-impressionist novel seemed strange and daring in 1918. That all action, even the most realistic situations, should be sifted ostensibly through the consciousness of the protagonist before being transferred to the page by the author meant an alteration in the task of the reader. The author, no longer omniscient and omnipresent, was now bound to record only what impressed itself as significant on the mind and emotions of his central character. If that meant a gap of three years here, five years there, in the action, so be it. The author had to restrain his wish to tell all, to aid his audience with Dickensian asides. He had to become in theory merely the instrument of the hero he had created. Actually, it goes without saying, the success of each such experiment in fiction varied directly with the skill and the sensitivity of the author in manipulating his protagonist so that, out of the welter of raw impressions that go into mak-

Excerpted from *Joyce: The Man, the Work, the Reputation,* by Marvin Magalaner and Richard M. Kain (New York: New York University Press, 1956). Reprinted with permission.

ing an existence, the novel should highlight those best calculated to provide significant fictional form. It was Joyce's talent to do this surpassingly well.

The method of impressionism may be dangerous in its tendency to encourage vague outlines and absence of clear pattern. If the consciousness of a human, and therefore imperfect, protagonist is to be taken as the touchstone of relevance in a fictional work, then the work may theoretically wander as far afield in its structure and substance as the vagaries of its fallible hero. To replace the comfortable, traditional mold of chronological narration of objectively recorded events, the author must find a device which, while it does not violate the impressionist stream, will provide a measure of cohesion, continuity, and firmness in which discrete impressions merge to become pervasive themes.

### THE MOTIF IS JOYCE'S DEVICE

Joyce's device in *A Portrait* is the motif—the expressive reiteration of an action, a situation, or a speech, which eventuates in the emergence of a significant pattern of meaning or feeling essential to the unity of the novel. Sometimes the motif is scarcely noticeable, and yet it operates below the threshold of awareness. At other times the motif may be insistently present in the consciousness of the reader (*i.e.*, the red and the green imagery of the first chapter) without the reader knowing precisely what to make of the theme or what to do with it. Certain motifs, finally, clear in their significance, frequent in their occurrence, need little critical exegesis to be felt and understood by the average reader.

[Critic] Hugh Kenner, in his excellent article, "The Portrait in Perspective," points out that the motifs introduced on the first page or so of the book contain the germ of all that Joyce had to say in *A Portrait* and in each of his subsequent novels. To trace one of these motifs in its various appearances through the book should demonstrate its value in cementing together the often discontinuous narrative blocks.

### ONE MOTIF TRACED IN SEVERAL EPISODES

Joyce introduces the motif on page two:

> When they were grown up he was going to marry Eileen.
> He hid under the table. His mother said:
> —O, Stephen will apologise.
> Dante said:

—O, if not, the eagles will come and pull out his eyes.—

> Pull out his eyes,
> Apologise,
> Apologise,
> Pull out his eyes.

Thus, even in early childhood, Stephen is revealed as guilty of an unspecified crime possibly related to sex (". . . he was going to marry Eileen") or to religion (Eileen is a Protestant) or simply to disobedience of constituted authority (his mother and his governess). Authority demands that he admit the alleged error of his way or suffer the painful consequences. In this first reference to the motif, as Kenner mentions, Prometheus is undoubtedly suggested: first, because of his awful torment at the hands of the authority he had defied (Stephen's eyes are more vulnerable than his liver, so the Promethean punishment undergoes alteration); second, because in stealing fire from the gods, Prometheus performs literally Stephen-Joyce's later act of taking creative inspiration from its mysterious source. So much for the initial statement of the motif.

Only two paragraphs later, a variation of the motif is presented. Stephen, at Clongowes, is questioned by an older boy, Nasty Roche:

What is your name?
Stephen had answered: Stephen Dedalus.
Then Nasty Roche had said:
—What kind of a name is that?
And when Stephen had not been able to answer Nasty Roche had asked:
—What is your father?
Stephen had answered:
—A gentleman.
Then Nasty Roche had asked:
—Is he a magistrate?

This sharp question and answer routine, suggesting in its definiteness a familiar catechism, reinforces the motif of apology for a hazy guilt that outsiders feel Stephen ought to exhibit. Always troubled by questions about his father in later boyhood, he is even at this early period brought to the point at which he must remain silent or confess that his father is not what he might be—a keenly felt reflection on the young boy himself. It is interesting, considering Joyce's care in selecting names for his characters, that Roche ("rock," in French) may well represent the church here putting the questions—and a "Nasty" Roche at that.

Several pages further on, Stephen again feels a sense of sin and guilt when questioned by Wells on whether he kisses his mother every night before he goes to bed. The "other fellows" laugh when he says that he does and redouble their laughter when, in confusion, he says that he does not. Once more, the little boy feels guilty when society singles him out for questioning, scorn, and ridicule. He "blushed under their eyes" and wondered, "What was the right answer to the question? He had given two and still Wells laughed." In the climactic scene of Chapter 1, Stephen is questioned by Father Dolan, here the actual representative of the Catholic Church, and then punished for a crime of which he is innocent—a crime, to reinforce the motif, that involves punishment for having weak eyes. When summoned from his seat in the classroom to be beaten by Dolan, Stephen stumbles, "blinded" by fear and haste. At the blow of the pandybat upon his hand, "A cry sprang to his lips, a prayer to be let off. But . . . he held back the hot tears and the cry that scalded his throat." Stephen, the embryo artist and rebel, will not "Apologise" even when the world seeks to "Pull out his eyes." Stephen kneels on the floor, ironically out of fear and pain inflicted by the father rather than from adoration. He has not knuckled under to the pressures of his hostile environment.

Numerous further instances of the pervasiveness of this motif might be adduced, but two or three additional examples should suffice. In high school at Belvedere, Stephen's schoolmates twit him about his ascetic ways, his father, and his girl friend. When he does not readily confess his latest love affair, he is playfully hit with Heron's cane until he jestingly recites the *Confiteor*[1] to the reiterated beat of the admonition, "Admit." These same "friends" belabor him, more in seriousness than in jest, for refusing to allow, in a literary catechism, that "Byron was no good." Again he is tormented, like St. Stephen[2] by the mob, for sticking to his beliefs. Again, the refrain is "Admit." To avoid an open clash, he is forced to confess his error in theology on an English composition, when questioned by Mr. Tate. Most dramatic, perhaps, is Stephen's confession to the old priest of his sins of the flesh—a terrified outburst occasioned by the long, dreadful sermon on Hell, which develops in macrocosm the motif of "Apologise/Pull out his eyes" enunciated in microcosm at the beginning of *A Portrait.*

---

1. confession   2. In the New Testament story Stephen was stoned.

With powerful motifs such as this—or the theme of mother-lover-church or exile and flight or the religion of art and the dedication of the artist—running through the book to give it substance and form, there is little need for the step-by-step nursing that [British novelists John] Galsworthy or Arnold Bennett so skillfully supplied for their readers. Relatively few in *A Portrait*, and comparatively simple, these themes increase and multiply, twine and intertwine, to form the narrative meshes of *Ulysses* and the *Wake*. The intellectually apprehended motifs of his *Portrait* become the elaborate musical and rhythmical and multi-leveled symbolic fabric of Joyce's maturer works.

Yet it is not too much to say that even in *A Portrait*, as in *Dubliners*—both preparatory exercises for the books to follow—the author left little to chance. The marks of his consummate control are evident in every line. From the name of Betty Byrne (compounded of Elizabeth as mother of John the Baptist and of Byrne, real name of Cranly, who in *A Portrait* is identified as the precursor) to the characterization of Simon Moonan as toady, no name or fact seems too unimportant to escape Joyce's obsession for total relevance. One case in point demonstrates how this compulsion may work toward the strengthening of a key motif.

## THE SIGNIFICANCE OF THE PLAY *THE LADY OF LYONS*

Near the end of Chapter 2 of *A Portrait*, Joyce makes the offhand remark that with "the money of his [school] prizes," Stephen Dedalus "led a party of three or four to the theater to see . . . *The Lady of Lyons*." This is the first and last mention of [British playwright and novelist Edward] Bulwer-Lytton's play in the book, although the name of the main character of the romance appears once, two pages farther on. A synopsis of the plot of this casually mentioned play gives little hint of the use to which it is to be put by Joyce. Pauline Deschappelles, a proud beauty, scorns marriage for money or for the sake of acquiring a title. Her rejected suitors plot to humble her by tricking her into marriage with a social inferior, Claude Melnotte, the son of a gardener. Melnotte, just returned from Paris where his father's legacy has allowed him to learn Latin, dancing, fencing, and the other arts, is the darling of the village. Though he wears fine clothes and looks like a prince, he hides his love for Pauline because he is conscious of his social handicap as a gardener's son. He watches his unattainable heroine from afar, sends her flowers anonymously, and finally dares to send her his poetry, which she rejects violently.

Insulted, Claude joins the conspiracy to force Pauline to wed beneath her station. She falls into the trap, but before the marriage his true love for her makes him unwilling to carry the plot to its end. His cohorts, the rejected suitors, insist, and the two are joined. Pauline discovers the fraud, spurns his attentions, and is allowed to retain her virtue. After several further turns of the plot, Claude goes off to battle to forget his part in the shameful affair. He returns rich and powerful several years later to find Pauline about to marry one of the suitors in order to save her father from bankruptcy. Having made his fortune in the wars, Claude is able to pay the debt, save his love from a fate worse than death, take revenge on the wicked suitors, and carry off the prize as the curtain comes down.

### THE CONNECTION BETWEEN THE PLAY AND THE NOVEL *THE COUNT OF MONTE CRISTO*

This is as unlikely a story with which to fortify a motif as one can find for an author who, above all, abhorred the sentimental and the banal. But just as Joyce found use in the Nausicaä episode of *Ulysses* for such a mood as a foil for the contrasting mood of Leopold Bloom, so in *A Portrait* Bulwer-Lytton's play has its appropriate place.

Joyce had used the motif of the unworthy adolescent lover before in the "Araby" story of *Dubliners*. There the boy narrator watches his beloved from afar, not daring to submit the ideality of his illusion to the soiled world of reality. In that story also there is the desire to bear gifts to his love—to seek adventure so that he may be worthy. In "Araby" Joyce hints at the ideal love of Dante for the ideal abstraction of Beatrice.

In *A Portrait*, the motif suggested by *The Lady of Lyons* is subordinate to, but on a plane parallel with, the theme of *The Count of Monte Cristo*. The latter serves as one of the unifying threads of the impressionist narrative. Its motif deserves separate treatment, which cannot be offered here except in brief allusion. Stephen is shown poring over a "ragged translation of *The Count of Monte Cristo*," which stamps firmly in his mind the "figure of that dark avenger" and of his secret lover, Mercedes, always pictured thereafter as standing in a garden. Stephen's adolescent identification with this avenging shadow, with this heroic lover-adventurer, leads to childish fantasies in which he sees himself a dignified and proud lover, able to refuse with haughtiness and restraint the tribute of Mercedes, "who had so many years before slighted his love." He revels in his imaginary response, "Madam, I never eat muscatel grapes." The restlessness induced by the drab routine of growing up in Dublin sends him "wandering in the evening from garden to garden in search of Mercedes."

The reinforcement of the Monte Cristo theme by *The Lady of Lyons* motif is clear. In both, and for all of Joyce's adolescent heroes, there is the unapproachable heroine against a background of gardens and flowers; the lover whose sense of inferiority prevents him from speaking out; the eventual acquiring of polish, of Continental culture and wealth (or the hope of such acquisition); the turning of the tables that gives the mature lover the opportunity to show his true worth by rescuing the now chastened heroine from difficulty and to "play the dark avenger" to his enemies.

It is obvious that Joyce expected such parallels as have been pointed out to be apparent to his readers. Both the play and the book enjoyed wide popularity among the middle classes in the nineteenth century. An indication of his being able to take this for granted is offered by the casual mention of Bulwer-Lytton's hero, Claude Melnotte, with no further reference to the source from which the hero was being drawn:

> Only at times, in the pauses of his desire, when the luxury that was wasting him gave room to a softer languor, the image of Mercedes traversed the background of his memory. He saw again the . . . garden of rosebushes . . . and he remembered the sadly proud gesture of refusal which he was to make there, standing with her in the moonlit garden after years of estrangement and adventure. At those moments the soft speeches of Claude Melnotte rose to his lips and eased his unrest. A tender premonition touched him of the tryst he had then looked forward to and, in spite of the horrible reality which lay between his hope of then and now, of the holy encounter he had then imagined at which weakness and timidity and inexperience were to fall from him.

It is also apparent how inextricably bound up are the two motifs in Joyce's own mind, so that Melnotte and Monte Cristo are interchangeable symbols of a state of feeling.

These "soft speeches" of Claude Melnotte offer considerable further reasons for Joyce's selection of *The Lady of Lyons* as the play to which Stephen, in *A Portrait,* should take his parents and friends. Claude's mother in the play, suspicious of her son's cultural acquisitions from the Continent and of his unorthodox artistic bent, nags him constantly to abandon the ways of the artist and return to honest, normal, lucrative pursuits:

> Leave glory to great folks. Ah! Claude, Claude! Castles in the air cost a vast deal to keep up! How is all this to end? What good does it do thee to learn Latin, and sing songs, and play on the guitar, and fence and dance, and paint pictures? All very fine; but what does it bring in?

Though slightly more florid than the speeches of Stephen's mother, bidding him beware of dangerous authors like Ibsen and urging him to accept a job in Guinness' respectable brewery, these quoted remarks in the play must have carried a familiar note to mother and son. And Claude's "soft" answer is, though embroidered and dated, what we should have expected Stephen to say:

> Wealth! wealth, my mother!—wealth to the mind—wealth to the heart—high thoughts—bright dreams—the hope of fame—the ambition to be worthier to love Pauline.

Melnotte's passion for Pauline follows the same pattern as Stephen's for his succession of dream lovers. First he wrestles with an inferiority complex: "Even from this low cell, poverty,—I lift my eyes to Pauline and forget my chains." Then follows the association of the loved one with flowers. "Thou knowest not that for the last six weeks I have sent every day the rarest flowers to Pauline; she wears them. I have seen them on her breast. . . ." Finally, emboldened by apparent success, Melnotte, like Stephen, composes poetry for the lady: "I have now grown more bold—I have poured my worship into poetry—I have sent my verses to Pauline I have signed them with my own name." Moreover, while Stephen ordinarily does not take overt action to achieve his aim in love, and therefore feels himself defeated, Melnotte, because he takes the step, is rejected utterly.

Yet, despite Joyce's deliberate emphasis on these superficial similarities, Stephen certainly is following a path basically different from the one traversed by such romantic heroes as Melnotte. The irony of the surface comparison, as Professor Charles Anderson has pointed out to the present writer, is underlined by the dissimilar character of their respective dream worlds. Melnotte can push his luck, can hope eventually to get the girl of his feverish dreams, the *ne plus ultra*[3] of his worldly hopes. For Stephen the dream world is dissipated even as it takes form. The woman figure, whether Mercedes or another, is unattainable both as a flesh and blood person and as symbolic representation of the church, beckoning him to intimate communion through the sacramental "muscatel grapes," which he must refuse.

Melnotte, Dante, Stephen, Joyce, Monte Cristo—all these figures merge at times, at other times stand apart and operate separately to achieve the literary ends of the author. The story of Stephen's boyhood could have been told without the frequent iteration of parallel motifs. The recognition of such motifs, however, affords to the reader a control of the narrative, both intellectual and emotional, impossible in single-leveled fiction. Understanding this, Joyce strives to make every word count, both for itself and for the surrounding context.

3. nothing more beyond

# The Bird Motif

Weldon Thornton

Weldon Thornton analyzes the bird motif in three stages. In the first stage he presents the motif as a combination of three negative elements. In the second stage Thornton analyzes the turning point when Stephen redesigns the image into a positive symbol of his own destiny. Finally Thornton shows that even the recast image of the bird has uneasy and fearful undertones. Weldon Thornton teaches English at the University of North Carolina in Chapel Hill. He is the author of *Allusions in "Ulysses": An Annotated List* and *J.M. Synge and the Western Mind,* and coeditor (with Robert Newman) of *Joyce's "Ulysses": The Larger Perspective.*

In *Portrait of the Artist,* to a degree that is perhaps unique, the structures of the novel and the complexes of Stephen's mind are so fully identified that every motif is simultaneously aesthetic/structural and psychological.

The bird motif is appropriate for my purpose for several reasons. For one, the meanings the image takes on as the novel progresses involve a subtle blend of "inner" and "outer" factors—i.e., of Stephen's "inherent" attitude toward the image, and of negative associations surrounding his early experiences with the image. The motif first appears on the second page of the novel, in an ambiguous but fearful, emotion-charged context that dictates its meaning for Stephen for some time to come. There is evidence later in the novel that Stephen's innate disposition toward the image of the bird is positive, but so strongly negative is its original experiential context that the positive connotations the image has for him cannot manifest themselves in Stephen's psyche until much later. . . . Another point of interest in the bird image is Stephen's attempt self-consciously to reconstitute the meaning of the image for himself at a crucial point in his

Excerpted from *The Antimodernism of Joyce's* Portrait of the Artist as a Young Man, by Weldon Thornton. Copyright ©1994 by Syracuse University Press. Reprinted with permission from the publisher.

life—the climactic scene on the beach in chapter IV. The motif also permits us to see how subtly various conscious and subconscious dimensions of the image ramify in Stephen's psyche. That is, while certain instances of the motif establish clear-cut meanings and associations, radiating from these are others in which the image exerts subconscious influence in Stephen's mind.

Let us consider the original context of this motif:

> The Vances lived in number seven. They had a different father and mother. They were Eileen's father and mother. When they were grown up he was going to marry Eileen. He hid under the table. His mother said:
> —O, Stephen will apologize.
> Dante said:
> —O, if not, the eagles will come and pull out his eyes.
>
> > *Pull out his eyes,*
> > *Apologize,*
> > *Apologize,*
> > *Pull out his eyes.*
>
> > *Apologize,*
> > *Pull out his eyes,*
> > *Pull out his eyes,*
> > *Apologize.*

### THE BIRD IMAGE: A COMPLEX OF THREE ELEMENTS

The context here involves certain meanings and connotations that recur in subsequent occurrences of the motif—that become a complex, in the Jungian sense of the term. The main elements of this complex are 1) accusation and threat of punishment for something that Stephen does not fully understand or is not in fact guilty of; 2) the involvement of his eyes; and 3) the presence of the bird image. The vagueness in this episode about what Stephen must apologize for is probably a reflection of his own puzzlement about his "crime." Since Eileen is a girl and there is reference to marriage, and since she is (as we learn later) a Protestant, his offense may involve nascent sexuality, or religion. But precisely what the offense is we do not know, nor does Stephen. What is crucial is that the bird is forcibly presented to him as an instrument of punishment for some vaguely understood offense, and that the threat involves his eyes.

Throughout the first four chapters of the novel, this complex reoccurs with considerable integrity: the presence of certain elements of the complex is usually sufficient to trigger the whole. The next instance occurs on this same page, though separated from it in time by several years. Stephen is a very young boy at Clongowes, and we are told of his reluctance to take part in the rough sports that the others play:

> The wide playgrounds were swarming with boys. All were shouting and the prefects urged them on with strong cries. The evening air was pale and chilly and after every charge and thud of the footballers the greasy leather orb flew like a heavy bird through the grey light. He kept on the fringe of his line, out of sight of his prefect, out of the reach of the rude feet, feigning to run now and then. He felt his body small and weak amid the throng of players and his eyes were weak and watery.

This brief passage contains the elements of the complex—Stephen feels guilty about not taking part in the games, and so he feigns to run and tries to avoid the glance of the authority figure who would doubtless upbraid (perhaps even punish) him for his reluctance. Obviously he feels inadequate and vulnerable, and the reference to his bodily weakness focuses specifically on his "weak and watery eyes." The context here of Stephen's feelings of inadequacy and vague guilt make it appropriate that the ball should appear to Stephen as a bird—thus completing the complex and objectifying the nascent fear of punishment that he feels.

### EXPLICIT AND IMPLICIT EXAMPLES OF THE BIRD IMAGE COMPLEX

The episode most fully manifesting this complex is the pandybatting scene. Once again certain elements of the complex are literally present and others are projected into the experience by Stephen. Stephen is accused of something of which he is not guilty, and the purported crime involves his eyes: he is accused of having broken his glasses so that he will not have to do his lessons. Moreover, the description of Father Dolan, the punisher, invokes the image of an avenging eagle:

> Stephen lifted his eyes in wonder and saw for a moment Father Dolan's whitegrey not young face, his baldy whitegrey head with fluff at the sides of it, the steel rims of his spectacles and his nocoloured eyes looking through the glasses.

Here again, Stephen views Father Dolan as a bald eagle because the other elements of the complex suggest such a perception. In this context of vaguely understood guilt and fear, once again involving his eyes, it is natural that the punisher be seen as a bird. But the words *bird* or *eagle* are not present in the text, suggesting that the image may not be "consciously" present in Stephen's mind.

Other contexts in the early chapters of the novel involve a bird (or bird imagery) associated with fear. Stephen's apprehension about the "bird here waiting for you" he finds in the center of the dining room table at Christmas cannot be fully assuaged by his reassuring himself that his father purchased the turkey in Dunns of D'Olier Street, in part because of the unhappy coincidence that Mr. Barrett at Clongowes calls the instrument of punishment a turkey—though he tries by thinking, "but Clongowes was far away."

Another instance of the motif occurs in the episode with Heron, of whom Stephen "had often thought it strange that Vincent Heron had a bird's face as well as a bird's name." Appropriately the situation involves both accusation and punishment, in that Heron asks Stephen to "Admit" to having a girl friend (a dubious accusation of a noncrime) and strikes Stephen with a cane. And while this episode does not seriously disturb Stephen, it calls to his mind an earlier episode that he had found painful. In the wake of Mr. Tate's having accused Stephen of heresy (once again a "crime" of which he was not really guilty), Heron and others had taken the opportunity to attack the "heretic" and punish him over his refusal to disavow his admiration for Byron.

Other instances of the bird image or its associations seem not to rise fully to the surface in Stephen's mind—i.e., they are not explicit in the novel's language. Consider, for example, the sound associated with the flapping of the brothers' soutanes.[1] The sound is first referred to on the day of Stephen's arrival at Clongowes; just as his parents are leaving, there is a reference to the rector's "soutane fluttering in the breeze." While this phrase offers no confirmation as to whether the fluttering of the winglike soutane evokes in the boy's mind an image of a bird, conditions conducive to the bird-complex are present: the young boy, just separating, from his parents, is in a state of apprehension, perhaps even guilt, about his timidity and his wishing to be back at home, and the rector is for him a figure of awesome authority. Also, the sound of the soutane figures prominently in the pandybatting scene, where we are three times told that Stephen heard "the swish of the

---

1. ankle-length garments worn by the clergy and others assisting in church services

sleeve of the soutane as the pandybat was lifted to strike." But even though the context provided by the description of Father Dolan would readily support it, no explicit associa- tion of this sound with a bird is made at this point. But in a later passage the association of the soutane with a bird's wings is explicit; we are told that "the excited prefect was hustling the boys through the vestry like a flock of geese, flapping the wings of his soutane"—which suggests that ornithic associations were unconsciously present in the earlier instances of this image. . . .

## STEPHEN REDESIGNS THE BIRD IMAGE

The turning point in regard to this image comes at the end of the fourth chapter, when, as a part of his self-assertive re- definition of himself—his soul's arising from the grave of boyhood—Stephen reconstrues the image, in terms more appropriate to his own wishes. The result is that this image which always had connotations of fear and guilt is remade into an image of beauty and of his destiny. This change is ex- pressed both in his reflections on the figure of Daedalus, whose name he bears, and in his apprehension of the wad- ing girl. During the scene on the strand, Stephen thinks ex- plicitly of his strange name, and it seems to him "a prophecy." Of Daedalus, we are told,

> Now, at the name of the fabulous artificer, he seemed to hear the noise of dim waves and to see a winged form flying above the waves and slowly climbing the air. What did it mean? Was it a quaint device opening a page of some medieval book of prophecies and symbols, a hawklike man flying sunward above the sea, a prophecy of the end he had been born to serve and had been following through the mists of childhood and boyhood, a symbol of the artist forging anew in his work- shop out of the sluggish matter of the earth a new soaring im- palpable imperishable being?
>
> His heart trembled; his breath came faster and a wild spirit passed over his limbs as though he were soaring sun- ward. His heart trembled in an ecstasy of fear and his soul was in flight. His soul was soaring in an air beyond the world and the body he knew was purified in a breath and delivered of incertitude and made radiant and commingled with the el- ement of the spirit. An ecstasy of flight made radiant his eyes and wild his breath and tremulous and wild and radiant his windswept limbs.

In this passage the winged form flying above the waves is not an image of punishment but of freedom and release; the image Stephen thinks of here—hawk rather than eagle—is not one foisted upon him by intimidating authority, but one of his own making, his own imagining. His "eyes" participate in the transformation, both in that he "sees" the winged form climbing the air, and that his once weak and vulnerable eyes are now "radiant."

The girl is described in a variety of avian terms, all of them connoting beauty rather than threat:

> She seemed like one whom magic had changed into the likeness of a strange and beautiful seabird. Her long slender bare legs were delicate as a crane's and pure save where an emerald trail of seaweed had fashioned itself as a sign upon the flesh. Her thighs, fuller and softhued as ivory, were bared almost to the hips where the white fringes of her drawers were like featherings of soft white down. Her slateblue skirts were kilted boldly about her waist and dovetailed behind her. Her bosom was as a bird's soft and slight, slight and soft as the breast of some darkplumaged dove.

Clearly the image of the bird is no longer associated with fear and guilt and punishment; Stephen has remade the meaning of the image for himself into something far more positive—into an image of the beauty of the natural world and a promise of flight and of release.

The change that takes place here in Stephen's apprehension of the bird image is simply one part of a larger metamorphosis at this climactic point of the novel, because in Stephen's mind this is the juncture in his life at which he ceases to be dictated to by circumstance and becomes self-defining. . . . For the first four chapters of the novel, Stephen felt himself a passive victim of the meanings of the image that were branded into his psyche as a child. But at this climactic point of the novel, Stephen remakes the meaning of this image and of others. This confirms that this climactic event involves not simply his realization of his artistic calling, but his determination to take charge of his destiny, to become not the passive recipient of experience but the initiator.

This change in Stephen's sense of the bird image does carry over into chapter V, in that the bird images that occur there are associated with escape or release or with augury[2] or destiny. When talking with Davin, Stephen makes the statement that "when the soul of a man is born in this country there are nets flung at it to hold it back from flight. You

2. a sign of something to come; an omen

talk to me of nationality, language, religion. I shall try to fly by those nets." Here Stephen himself invokes the bird image (rather than having it pressed upon him by frightening circumstances) and presents it as an image of escape and freedom. Later, while standing on the steps of the library, he sees the birds flying around the house at the corner of Molesworth Street; he sees them as birds of augury, and he thinks again of "the hawklike man whose name he bore."

## THE NEW BIRD IMAGE IMPLIES UNEASE AND FEAR

But even into these newly-projected images of the bird, there creeps an undertone of unease and fear. The birds of augury, for example, are said to sound "like the squeak of mice behind the wainscot: a shrill twofold note," and though he tells himself "but the notes were long and shrill and whirring, unlike the cry of vermin," we must wonder whether the sound does not recall to him an image evoked by the retreat sermon: "The wind of the last day blew through his mind; his sins, the jeweleyed harlots of his imagination, fled before the hurricane, squeaking like mice in their terror and huddled under a mane of hair"—the only other mention of mice in the novel. Another note of unease in regard even to the image of the "hawklike man" is sounded a few paragraphs further on in the augury scene, when we are told "a sense of fear of the unknown moved in the heart of his weariness, a fear of symbols and portents, of the hawklike man whose name he bore soaring out of his captivity on osierwoven wings." Stephen may not have exorcised the fearful aspects of the bird image as fully as he thinks.

This same implication surfaces in the final instance of bird imagery in the novel—one of particular relevance to the theme of self-awareness and self-determination. The bird imagery of the closing paragraphs has implications Stephen himself seems unaware of and would probably be taken aback by. In the April 16 diary entry, Stephen thinks of certain enticing figures as "shaking the wings of their exultant and terrible youth," and then in the final sentence of the novel, he again invokes the figure of Daedalus, who was so important to his redefinition of the bird image. But here the invocation is significantly different, for in saying "old father, old artificer, stand me now and ever in good stead," Stephen is implicitly identifying himself with the son, Icarus. The image of flight, then, while still freed from the negative connotations that it had for the younger Stephen, is nonetheless more complex and more ominous than he realizes, for here at the very outset of his flight to freedom and self-realization, it forebodes a fall. Probably if Stephen were queried on this point—on why he has identified himself with the son rather than the father—he would deny any such implication, or certainly any such intention on his part. But the implication is there, and it has tonal and thematic appropriateness, in that it reveals how much more complex Stephen's psyche is than he himself realizes. . . .

I have focused on this motif because it illustrates that Stephen's psyche is more complex than he can realize, and that his sense of self-determination is exaggerated. This is shown first of all by the bird image entering into the psyche of the young Stephen in ways that he has virtually no awareness of, quite subconsciously. Also, the major change of meaning the image undergoes occurs at that climactic point when Stephen feels that he comes into control of his own destiny, redefining the bird image into one of Daedalian flight to freedom. But even this redefinition of the image is not completely within Stephen's conscious control, as the ironic implications of the final sentence of the novel show. Intending to cast himself as Daedalus, he unwittingly—perhaps under the influence of the negative connotations that the image so long held for him—casts himself as Icarus, expressing a subconscious sense that his flight to freedom is not so secure as he would like to believe.

# Joyce's Interconnecting Images

William York Tindall

William York Tindall maintains that Joyce's images enrich the prose and prepare the reader for Stephen's moments of realization. Tindall analyzes and links shifting images of roads, roses, girls, birds, bats, and water, that give the story texture and meaning. William York Tindall, one of the first American critics to study Joyce, taught English at Columbia University in New York. He is the author of *James Joyce: His Way of Interpreting the Modern World*, *A Reader's Guide to James Joyce*, and *The Joyce Country*.

Joyce's images, though partly assigned, however deliberate, are suggestive, indefinite, and not altogether explicable. Ambivalent, they reveal not only the quality of experience but its complexity. Without attendant or essential images, *A Portrait of the Artist* would be so much less immediate and less moving that few would pick it up again.

Images play other parts in the great design. Embodying Stephen's experience before he is entirely aware of it, and doing the same service for us, they prepare for moments of realization, which could not occur without them. Operating below conscious notice, the images, rhythms, and other forms project an unconscious process that comes to light at last. This function is no more important, however, than that of relating part to part and, composing a structure which, with the dominant narrative it supplements and complicates, creates what Stephen calls radiance or the meaning of the composite form.

The first two pages of *A Portrait of the Artist* present the images that, when elaborated, are to compose the supplementary structure and take their place in the form. We are

Excerpted from *The Literary Symbol*, by William York Tindall (Bloomington: Indiana University Press, 1965). Copyright ©1955 by Columbia University Press. Reprinted with permission from Columbia University Press via the Copyright Clearance Center, Inc.

confronted here with a moocow coming down the road, with a rose (maybe green), with wetting the bed, with a girl, and with an eagle that plucks out eyes—not to mention a number of other things such as dancing to another's tune. Without much context as yet, these images, acquiring fresh meanings from recurrence and relationship with others, carry aspects of Stephen and his trouble. Never was opening so dense as this or more important.

## THE ROAD

Take that road, long, narrow, and strictly bounded, along which comes a moocow to meet the passive boy. Diction, rhythm, and the opening phrase (the traditional beginning of an Irish "story") suggest the condition of childhood and its helplessness. Confined to the road, the child cannot escape encounter with a creature traditionally associated with Irish legend and with everything maternal. Later, Stephen delights to accompany the milkman in his round of neighboring roads, although a little discouraged by the foul green puddles of the cowyard. Cows, which have seemed so beautiful in the country on sunny days, now revolt him and he can look no longer at their milk. Yet as he pursues "the Rock Road," he thinks a milkman's life pleasant enough, and looks forward with equanimity to adopting it as his own. Innumerable connotations of word and phrase make it almost plain at last that the road suggests tradition, that the cow suggests church, country, and all maternal things, and that the milkman suggests the priest. The little episode, far from being a sign of these meanings, is no more than the embodiment of possibilities. What it implies awaits corroboration from later episodes, Stephen's rejection of the priesthood, for example, or his aesthetic query about the man hacking a cow by accident from a block of wood. It is certain that none of these connected images is casual. As for the road itself, it develops into the circular track round which Mike Flynn, the old trainer, makes Stephen run; into the track at Clongowes where Stephen, breaking his glasses, is almost blinded; into the dark road alongside which Davin meets his peasant woman; and, after many reappearances, all of which confirm and enlarge the initial idea and feeling of tradition, into its opposite, the road that promises freedom on the final page.

## THE ROSE AND THE GIRL

The images of rose, water, girl, and bird are so intricately involved with one another that it seems all but impossible to separate them for analysis. Take the rose, however, a symbol which, carrying traditional significance, becomes, after much recurrence, Stephen's image of woman and creativity. Lacking sufficient context at its first appearance to have certain meaning, the rose, made green by Stephen, is not altogether without possibilities. Green is the color of Ireland, of immaturity, and of vegetable creation; yet a green rose is unnatural. Art is unnatural too. Could the green rose anticipate Stephen's immature desire for Irish art? We cannot tell for sure. At school Stephen is champion of the white rose that loses to the red in an academic war of roses; and during his period of "resolute piety" his prayers ascend to heaven "like perfume streaming upwards from a heart of white rose." It is the red rose, however, that attends his creative ecstasies near the Bull Wall, after he resolves to follow mortal beauty, and in bed, after composing a poem. His soul, "swooning into some new world," shares Dante's penultimate vision: "A world, a glimmer, or a flower? Glimmering and trembling, trembling and unfolding, a breaking light, an opening flower, it spread in endless succession to itself, breaking in full crimson and unfolding and fading to palest rose, leaf by leaf and wave of light by wave of light, flooding all the heavens with its soft flushes, every flush deeper than the other." This heavenly vision, which follows the hell of the sermons and the purgatory of his repentance, anticipates his ultimate vision of Mrs. Bloom, the heavenly yet earthly rose of *Ulysses*.

Woman, associated with rose, embodies Stephen's aspiration and, increasingly, his creative power. Eileen, the girl who appears at the beginning of the book, unattainable because Protestant, is soon identified with sex and the Tower of Ivory, symbol of the Blessed Virgin. Mercedes, a dream who inhabits a garden of roses along the milkman's road, suggests the Virgin by her name while adding overtones of remoteness, exile, and revenge. At Cork, however, Stephen's "monstrous" adolescent thoughts injure her purity by desire. When Emma, a teaser, replaces Mercedes as object of desire and becomes in addition an image of his mother country and his church, Stephen transfers his devotion to the Virgin herself, over whose sodality he presides, and whose "office" becomes his formula. The wading girl near the Bull Wall,

who embodies mortal beauty, unites all previous suggestions. Associating her with Emma, the Virgin, the rose, and
the womb of the imagination, whose priest he becomes, he
finds her an image of his own capacity: "Heavenly God!" his
soul exclaims, its eye no doubt upon himself. . . .

## THE COMMON GIRL AND THE KITCHEN GIRL

Other women take their place in the great design. There is
the common girl, persisting in memory, who stops Stephen
on the street to offer flowers for which he cannot pay. Connected in his mind with a kitchen girl who sings Irish
songs over the dishes, she develops near the end into the
servant maid, who, singing "Rosie O'Grady" in her kitchen,
proffers the suggestion at least of Irish flowers, green roses
perhaps. Cranly's *"Mulier cantat"*[1] unites her in Stephen's
mind with "the figure of woman as she appears in the
liturgy of the Church" and with all his symbolic women.
Unprepared as yet to receive what she proffers in her song
or unable to pay the price of acceptance, Stephen says, "I
want to see Rosie first."

That Rosie, another anticipation of Mrs. Bloom, sings in a
kitchen is not unimportant. After each of his ecstasies,
Stephen comes back to the kitchen, which serves not only as
an ironic device for deflating him but as an image of the reality to which, if he is to be an artist, he must return. . . .
Rosie in her kitchen, the last great image of woman in *A Portrait of the Artist*, unites the ideal with the actual. Neither the
wading girl nor Mercedes, both ethereal, can present to
Stephen the idea and feeling of a union which someday he
will understand. Far from seeing Rosie first, he sees her last,
but by her aid, of which he is not fully aware as yet, he
comes nearer his vision of above and below, of heavenly
roses to be sure but of roses in kitchens.

## BIRDS AND BATS

Woman is not only rose but bird and sometimes bat. The
bird, which makes its first appearance as the eagle who is to
punish Stephen's guilt by making him blind as a bat, makes
its next appearance as Heron, who, looking and acting like a
bird of prey, tries to make Stephen conform. Bad at first,
birds become good as Stephen approaches mortal beauty at

1. the woman sings

the beach. He thinks of Daedalus, "a hawklike man flying
sunward," and wants to utter cries of hawk or eagle, images
no longer of oppression but, retaining authority, of creation.
The wading girl is "a strange and beautiful seabird." "Her
bosom was as a bird's, soft and slight, slight and soft as the
breast of some darkplumaged dove." As Stephen observes
their flight, birds also become what he calls a "symbol of departure or loneliness." When, becoming birdlike Daedalus,
he takes flight across the sea to exile, he unites all these
meanings and confirms their association with water. Bats
are anticipated by images of blinding, not only those of the
eye-plucking eagle, of glasses broken on the track, and of
dull red blinds that keep light from boys of Belvedere during
their retreat but that of the woman into whose eye Mr. Casey
spits: "'Phth! says I to her.' 'O Jesus, Mary and Joseph!' says
she . . . 'I'm blinded and drownded . . . I'm blinded entirely.'"
When they appear at last, bats gather up these anticipatory
associations with woman, custom, and country. Davin's
peasant woman at her door along the dark lonely road
seems to Stephen "a type of her race and of his own, a bat-
like soul waking to the consciousness of itself in darkness
and secrecy and loneliness." Seeming almost a bird for a
moment, Emma, revisited, becomes another bat, but its
darkness, secrecy, and loneliness connect it with himself as
artist about to try silence, exile, and cunning. Blind to reality as yet, he may improve. Like the images of bird and
flower, the bat is ambivalent, not only bad but good. If bat
suggests things as they are, and bird things as they ought to
be, it is the artist's job to reconcile them. If all these women
are aspects of woman, and if woman is an aspect of himself,
the creative part, he too is presented by images of bird, bat,
and, besides these, water.

## WATER

Ambivalent from the first, water is either warm or cold,
agreeable or frightening. The making of water at the beginning of the *Portrait* seems an image of creation that includes the artist's two realities. At school Stephen is shouldered into the "square ditch," square not because of shape
but because it receives the flow of the urinal or "square."
Plainly maternal by context, this image warns Stephen of
the perils of regression, to which like one of those rats who
enjoy the ditch, he is tempted by the discomforts of exter-

nal reality. The "warm turf-coloured bogwater" of the bath adds something peculiarly Irish to his complex. Dirty water down the drain at the Wicklow Hotel and the watery sound of cricket bats (connected in his mind with pandy-bats and bats) confirm his fears. The concluding image of the first chapter, assigned only by previous associations, embodies his infantile career: "Pick, pack, pock, puck," go the cricket bats, "like drops of water in a fountain falling softly in the brimming bowl." If Stephen himself is suggested by this bowl and his development by an ablaut[2] series, water is not altogether bad. This possibility is established toward the middle of the book, where, changing character, water becomes good on the whole and unmistakably a symbol of creation. On his way to the beach, Stephen still finds the sea cold and "infra-human." The bathing boys repel him, but the sight of the wading girl gives water another aspect. Rolling up his trousers like J. Alfred Prufrock,[3] he himself goes wading. From that moment of baptism and rebirth inaudible music and the sound of waters attend his creative ecstasies. . . .

### THE FUNCTION OF FAMILIES OF IMAGES

These families of developing images that, supplementing the narrative, give it texture, immediacy, and more body are not the only symbolic devices Joyce commands. As we have noticed, large parallels, rhythms, shifts of tone, juxtaposition, and all else that [French novelist Gustave] Flaubert commended complicate the "significant form." But deferring these, I shall confine myself in this place to some of the relatively unassigned and unattached images that concentrate feeling at important points.

Consider, for example, the opening of the second chapter. Uncle Charles, who is addicted to black twist, is deported to the outhouse, whence rising smoke and the brim of his tall hat appear as he sings old songs in tranquillity. Position gives this image an importance that import cannot justify. Hints of exile, creation, and piety, all relevant to the theme, may divert our understanding without satisfying it entirely. Few of Joyce's images are so mysterious as this and, while occupying our feelings, so resistant to discourse. The

---

2. shifting vowel sounds, as in "pick, pack, pock, puck"   3. in T.S. Eliot's poem "The Lovesong of J. Alfred Prufrock"

scenery at Cork appeals more readily to the understanding. While in that town with his father, Stephen finds in the word "Foetus," carved in the wood of a desk, what [poet T.S.] Eliot would call an objective correlative of the "den of monstrous images" within him. After this corroboration of inner disorder, he emerges from the schoolroom into the sunny street where he sees cricketers and a maid watering plants; hears a German band and scale after scale from a girl's piano. In another book this urban noise and scenery might serve as setting alone. Here, more functional than that, it presents a vision of the normal, the orderly, and the quotidian from which the discovery of his monstrous interior has separated him.

## CHARACTERS

Characters are no less symbolic. The two dwarfish eccentrics that Stephen encounters, one on the street and the other in the library, seem caricatures of Stephen's possible future and of the soul of Ireland, but aside from that, they evade significance. By action, speech, and context, on the other hand, the figure of Cranly becomes more nearly definite. That last interview which drives Stephen to exile concentrates in Cranly the forces of admission, submission, confession, and retreat, and he becomes the embodiment of all that has plagued the imperfect hero. Cranly's preoccupation with a book called *Diseases of the Ox* adds to the picture. Since Stephen as "Bous Stephanoumenos" has been identified with the ox, Cranly's devotion to his book reveals him as Stephen's most reactionary critic, not, as we had supposed, his friend.

When Stephen turns seaward toward his great experience with the wading girl, an image which might escape casual notice not only suggests the finality of his action but adds to our understanding of his complexity: he crosses the bridge from Dollymount to the Bull. . . .

In the *Portrait,* on the bridge which marks his passage from old custom to freedom and the waters of life, he meets a squad of uncouth, tall-hatted Christian Brothers, marching two by two, going the other way. Their direction, their appearance, and their regimentation are important, but what reveals Stephen's character is the contempt with which he regards those who are socially and intellectually inferior to Jesuits. The episode, therefore, includes both his escape from one tyranny and his submission to another, the greater tyranny of pride, which, until he understands the Blooms, will keep him from uniting the regions of reality by art. Stephen may think of charity or Joyce talk of pride, but this revealing episode contributes more than all that talk or thought to the portrait of an artist.

# CHAPTER 5

# Joyce's Language

# Joyce's Multiple Writing Styles

Sydney Bolt

Sydney Bolt claims that no novel written before *A Portrait* can match its variety of styles. Bolt contrasts the dialogue of various characters with Stephen's own voice. According to Bolt, Joyce used distinctive styles to convey Stephen's tendency toward contemplation, identify the narrator as a reporter of information, and direct the reader's thoughts and understanding. Sydney Bolt taught English at Anglia Polytechic. He is the author of *Teaching Fiction in Schools.*

Where *A Portrait of the Artist as a Young Man* marks an advance on *Dubliners*[1] is in the use of sympathetic narrative styles. In the earlier work this was tentative. In the later work it predominates from the start. As the style of the opening of the story 'Clay' mimics Maria, the opening pages of the novel present the central character in what appears to be a record of his own childish prattle. As with Maria, however, so with Stephen, no occasion for the prattle is suggested. Despite its restricted style, it takes the form of third-person, not first-person narrative. Pastiche[2] continues to be used in this way throughout the novel. Its character inevitably alters as Stephen develops, especially because, from the second chapter onward, it is modelled on his reading rather than on his speech. The effect, however, remains. It suggests constraints.

Thus, at Clongowes:

> It made him very tired to think that way. It made him feel his head very big.

At Belvedere:

> A shaft of momentary anger flew through Stephen's mind at

---

1. James Joyce's collection of stories, published before *A Portrait*   2. fragments, ingredients, motifs from various sources; a hodgepodge

Excerpted from *A Preface to James Joyce*, 2nd ed., by Sydney Bolt (London: Longman, 1992). Reprinted by permission of Pearson Education Limited.

these indelicate allusions in the hearing of a stranger. For him there was nothing amusing in a girl's interest and regard.

At University College:

> It was the windless hour of dawn when madness wakes and strange plants open to the light and the moth flies forth silently.

The quotations do not of course imply that the narrative falls into three stages, with three corresponding styles. On the contrary, in each chapter the variations of Stephen's attitudes and moods call for several different styles. Never before had a novel been written in such a variety of different styles, and this fact is an indication of Joyce's originality. A more instructive clue to the nature of his genius, however, is the way in which style is thrust into the reader's face, as an object not for his admiration but for his critical inspection. Transparency was the last thing Joyce aimed for in style. He deliberately employed style as an obtrusive factor, claiming the reader's critical attention as an essential component of the understanding which the writing was intended to convey. Thus, in the passages quoted, the obtrusive features—the artlessness of the first, the stilted self-consciousness of the second, and the cosmetic aestheticism of the third—are there to be noticed. They are gestures expressing Stephen's state of mind, and they serve to focus attention on the limitations of that state of mind.

## CONTRASTS IN THE DIALOGUE

This variety is itself enough to provoke comparisons, but Joyce also provides material for more immediate contrast. One such ground for comparison is provided by the dialogue. Although the novel is written from Stephen's point of view, this does not prevent other characters from speaking for themselves. Indeed it is characteristic of Stephen to pay close attention to the way in which people speak. Side by side with passages written in styles sympathetic to Stephen we therefore find passages couched in alien styles. The most massive of these is the series of sermons in the third chapter. Other extended examples are Mr Casey's anecdote at the Christmas dinner, Simon Dedalus on many occasions but most notably his anecdote about his father, and Davin's anecdote about the village woman. All of these have their characteristic styles, which contrast with Stephen's. No less characteristic, and equally effective as background, are brief utterances such as bring to life the prefect of studies: 'lazy, idle little loafer'—the dean of studies: 'when may we expect to have something from you on the aesthetic question?'—or Cranly's 'let us eke go'. To these samples may be added the memorabilia that surround Stephen, like Napoleon's reply when asked what was the happiest day of his life: 'Gentlemen, the happiest day of my life was the day in which I made my first holy communion.'

When it occurs in discussions with Stephen, this alien speech inevitably produces a contrast with his own utterances. But it also serves for purposes of contrast when it interrupts passages of sympathetic narrative. Thus Stephen's fanciful response to a hellfire sermon

> He passed up the staircase and into the corridor along the walls of which the overcoats and waterproofs hung like gibbeted malefactors, headless and dripping and shapeless.

is juxtaposed with the more normal reactions of his classmates

> —I suppose he rubbed it into you well.
> —You bet he did. He put us all into a blue funk.

Similar effects are also, for example, produced in the fourth chapter, when juxtaposition emphasises the enervation of the style recording Stephen's reveries as he walks beside the sea.

> So timeless seemed the grey warm air, so fluid and impersonal his own mood, that all ages were as one to him. A moment before the ghost of the ancient kingdom of the Danes had looked forth through the vesture of the hazewrapped city. Now, at the name of the fabulous artificer, he seemed to hear the noise of dim waves and to see a winged form flying above the waves and slowly climbing the air. What did it mean? Was it a quaint device opening a page of some medieval book of prophecies and symbols, a hawklike man flying sunward above the sea, a prophecy of the end he had been born to serve and had been following through the mists of childhood and boyhood, a symbol of the artist forging anew in his workshop out of the sluggish matter of the earth a new soaring impalpable imperishable being?

The idiom of Stephen's boisterous fellows—Good man, Towser! Duck him!—offers a chastening contrast with the precious style in which his exotic flight of fancy is presented. It spotlights the complacency of 'his mild proud sovereignty'. Their derision invites the reader's complicity. The more closely the passage is read the more it reveals that Stephen's mood depends upon a refusal to see what is in front of him.

## A STYLE TO CONVEY STEPHEN'S REFLECTIVE NATURE

His perceptions are visionary and vague, marked by words like 'ghost', 'haze-wrapped', 'dim' and 'mists', and by the frequency of abstract terms like 'form', 'prophecies', 'symbol' and 'being'. The synthetic quality of the experience is also accentuated by the inclusion of words remote from common speech—'vesture', 'fabulous artificer', 'quaint device'. But, above all, the sentences lack thrust. They dwell rather than do. This effect is accentuated in the first sentence by inversion ('So timeless seemed . . .'), and in the last, long sentence by use of the interrogative form to conceal assertion. In both these sentences, also, an appositional structure delays progression. 'So timeless . . . so fluid . . .', 'Was it a quaint device . . . a hawk-like man . . . a prophecy . . . a symbol?'

The tendency of certain sentences to *dwell* rather than *do* is a recurrent feature of the prose throughout the novel. It registers a persistent feature of Stephen's mind—his contemplativeness. Once a perception has ignited his mind, it is deliberately held there until it fades away. This process is what Stephen, in his conversation with Lynch, calls 'the enchantment of the heart'. 'The mind in that mysterious instant Shelley likened to a fading coal.' Stylistically it is registered by a sequence of phrases in apposition—'like drops of water in a fountain falling softly in the brimming bowl.' The last sentence of the quotation, 'Was it a quaint device . . . ?', will serve as an example of this construction. It is long, but lacks the periodic effect of climax. It merely undulates and lingers. This construction has little use for the main verb, and can even dispense with it, as in this from the later journal: 'Faintly, under the heavy night, through the silence of the city which has turned from dreams to dreamless sleep as a weary lover whom no caresses move, the sound of hoofs upon the road.'

## THE STYLE OF THE NARRATOR'S REPORT

An even stronger contrast with this precious style than that afforded by the coarse language of the schoolboys is offered by a starkly objective report on the next page.

> He looked northward towards Howth. The sea had fallen below the line of seawrack on the shallow side of the breakwater and already the tide was running out fast along the foreshore. Already one long oval bank of sand lay warm and dry amid the wavelets. Here and there warm isles of sand gleamed above the shallow tide, and about the isles and around the long bank and amid the shallow currents of the beach were lightclad gayclad figures, wading and delving.

Instead of dwelling on an impression by indefinitely extending it, the sentences in this passage deliver their message in a business-like way, and stop as soon as they have done so. Besides being thus direct, they are lively, and their life depends upon finite forms of the verb. The vocabulary, also by way of contrast, is concrete and familiar.

Objective reports offer similar contrasts at other places, as at the conclusion of the Christmas dinner scene:

> Mr Casey struggled up from his chair and bent across the table towards her, scraping the air from before his eyes with one hand as though he were tearing aside a cobweb.

This simile clearly did not originate in Stephen's mind. Nor could Stephen have perceived, at the end of the scene, that the face he raised to see his father's tears was 'terror-stricken'. The narrator, therefore, is not restricting himself to the character's point of view, let alone his language.

## THE STYLE OF THE AUTHOR'S CONTROL

Although the novel is unusually dramatic, in that much of the story is told in characteristic dialogue and ironically sympathetic narrative prose, in places where the reader might expect reliable guidance Joyce does not scruple to assert his authority as author. The kind of narrative prose just quoted is one example of this process. So also is the inclusion in each chapter of at least one conclusive statement sign-posting the current direction of Stephen's development with a perspicacity which Stephen himself does not command. For example, we are told in the second chapter:

> The causes of his embitterment were many, remote and near. He was angry with himself for being young and the prey of restless foolish impulses, angry also with the change of fortune which was reshaping the world about him into a vision of squalor and insincerity. Yet his anger lent nothing to the vision.

What we have here is not an analysis of the boy's situation as he sees himself, but authorial guidance to assist our reading of the three epiphanies which immediately ensue.

Yet another means of authorial control, used consistently throughout the book, is the reiteration of key words. Sometimes such repetition, contributing to the rhythm of a paragraph, is an expression of Stephen's prolongation of the contemplative moment, as in the description of the wading girl—'But her long fair hair was girlish: and girlish, and touched with the wonder of mortal beauty, her face.' It is, however, also used in passages of objective background description, as in the passage quoted earlier in this section, describing the beach: the inviting repetition of 'already' and 'warm', and the insistent repetion of 'shallow'. The same device is extended to entire chapters: thus the words 'nice' and 'nasty' continuously recur in the first chapter, marking the poles of conformity and disobedience which plot Stephen's childhood during the Clongowes period. By an even more extended use of this device, key words like 'pride' and 'weariness' recur from chapter to chapter. More subtly, chapters are linked by repeatedly connecting a particular word and a particular sort of situation. Thus, in the quoted sentence describing Mr Casey's confrontation with Dante, he 'bent' across the table, just as in the anecdote he is about to tell, he 'bent down' to spit in the eye of a woman who confronted him in the road, and Stephen 'bent towards' the flower girl who stopped him in the street, and 'bent down' also to ask an old woman in the street the way to a chapel where he could make his confession. . . .

The story of the novel is the story of his encounters with reality, and all these encounters are verbal.

# Stephen's Language: A Clue to Joyce's Attitude

Robert M. Adams

Robert M. Adams acknowledges that Joyce did not make clear whether he intended the reader's attitude toward Stephen to be favorable or unfavorable, and suggests that Stephen's language offers a clue. Adams identifies Stephen's early awareness of story and poem, his curiosity about words at Clongowes, his manipulation of words in critical situations, and his ability to create and control his own universe with words. Adams suggests that this facility with language suggests respect for the artist and, thus, for Stephen. Robert M. Adams, who taught English at Columbia, Rutgers, and Cornell Universities, is the author of *The Texture of Joyce's* Ulysses, *Strains of Discord,* and *Ikon: John Milton and the Modern Critics.*

If the scenes of the novel [*Portrait*] are as discontinuous as loose beads, what strings them together? Primarily, of course, the development of Stephen Dedalus. On the stage of the novel, he always stands front and center. The portrait is of him, and the other characters are all ancillary; for example, only one of his siblings has so much as a name, that name is used only once, and as for the other young Dedaloi, we do not know even so much as their precise number (on p. 284 we get a very rough estimate). Stephen's central position is not automatic evidence that we are to take a favorable view of him; Sir Willoughby Patterne[1] occupies an equally central position in *The Egoist*. It does mean, however, that the word "hero" remains appropriate to him, and that the virtues or faults we impute to him cannot very well be mediocre ones. We see things through his eyes, we see very often only his reaction to things and not the things them-

1. a selfish and conceited character in George Meredith's novel

Excerpted from *James Joyce: Common Sense and Beyond,* by Robert M. Adams. Copyright ©1966 by Random House, Inc. Reprinted by permission of Random House, Inc.

selves, and this sort of focus, this continuous, detailed interest in the processes of his brain, renders it most unlikely that
he will prove to be such a flabby, floundering pseudo-artist
as Frederic Moreau, the protagonist of [French novelist Gus-
tave] Flaubert's *Sentimental Education* or the puppy who is
represented in [Anglo-Irish writer] George Moore's *Confessions of a Young Man.*

For example, a major theme in Joyce's description of his
literary artist's development is his growing command of
words and sensitivity to them. Even as a very young man indeed, Stephen is conscious of a story and a poem; and a momentary rhyme catches and fixes in his mind a connection
of far-reaching importance for the novel. The little boy who
crouches under the kitchen table reciting

> Pull out his eyes,
> Apologize,
> Apologize,
> Pull out his eyes.

is memorizing a connection between guilt, submission, and
weak eyesight, which, however irrational, could sink deep
into the mind of a sensitive child. The power of words to
hypnotize and fascinate is the least of the things demon-
strated in this abbreviated scene, which looks forward to a
whole series of demands for "submission'" somehow connected with weak eyesight and a bird which brings punishment from on high. (Cf. Father Dolan's descent on blinded
Stephen; the demand of Heron that he "admit"; his bitter
sense that sin comes through the eyes.)

## STEPHEN'S INTEREST IN WORDS AT CLONGOWES

At Clongowes too Stephen is shown to be permeated by
words and names. His own name is peculiar, and he does not
know "what kind of a name" it is; the word "belt" has a funny
double meaning; and the word "suck" has ugly, fascinating
connotations. Before long the suggestive power of words is
leading Stephen to compose, within his imagination, little romantic dramas in which he sees himself dying, the bell
tolling, farewell being said, a melancholy poem being re-
cited; and by a peculiar sort of confirmation, the vision of his
own funeral is repeated in the outside world by the funeral
of Parnell. This pattern seems, perhaps, over-ingenious and
arbitrary, but we know from outside sources how strong was
Joyce's identification with Parnell, and within the novel this

pattern recurs often enough and pointedly enough to have a serious claim on our attention. Words, for Stephen Dedalus, have a way of creating things; he thinks of the word, the symbol, first, then finds a confirmation of its existence, its meaning, in the outside world, or at least in an experience. Note how, though without the intervention of words, the green-maroon dichotomy of Dante's hairbrushes is confirmed in Fleming's coloring the earth green and the clouds maroon: "he had not told Fleming to colour them those colours. Fleming had done it himself." The tolling over and over of the words "dark," "cold," "pale," and "strange" produces a vision of Clongowes ghosts, specifically that Marshal Browne who had died at Prague in 1757. Or again the little song Stephen learned as a child:

> O, the wild rose blossoms
> On the little green place;

turns, in the presence of Father Arnall's division of the class into Yorkists (white roses) and Lancastrians (red roses) into a distortion, a vision of a new world.

> Lavender and cream and pink roses were beautiful to think of. Perhaps a wild rose might be like those colours and he remembered the song about the wild rose blossoms on the little green place. But you could not have a green rose. But perhaps somewhere in the world you could.

The sequence of thought here is deliberately indirect. Stephen's mind distorts the "natural" song into a pattern of words without referents, and finds in this world of imagery a sudden refuge from practical reality. Words, we will find if we look a little further ahead in the book,[2] are not simply passive or imitative devices for the artist; they are active tools with which he controls, modifies, and selects the raw materials of his life—and sometimes creating them.

A curious episode, involving another use of words, takes place while Stephen is in the infirmary at Clongowes. A boy named Athy points out to the slightly delirious Stephen that his name—Athy—is the name of a town, and then asks a riddle with a foolish answer: "Why is the county of Kildare like the leg of a fellow's breeches? . . . Because there is a thigh [Athy] in it." Then he tells Stephen you can ask the same riddle in another way. Stephen wants, mildly, to know what it is, but Athy won't tell, and he never does tell. Later, when

2. for example the poem "The Ivy whines upon the wall"

there is trouble in the school because some of the older boys have run away, Athy again has something to say; he has the inside story, and he tells it, bit by bit, always holding something back. They were caught—in the square—with Simon Moonan and Tusker Boyle—smugging. The point is not that this final word is a piece of insuperably recondite dialect, though plainly it is esoteric to young Stephen; it is the mysterious way in which language can be used to conceal as well as reveal (and the immense dimensions of a verbal mystery) which fascinates the embryo artist. And perhaps he is made aware, as well, that there are topics which society will not let us talk about distinctly—crevasses of conduct as well as of language, which open under our feet.

## WORDS ASSOCIATED WITH TRAUMATIC EXPERIENCES

A special development of these early pages is Stephen's habit of cradling a traumatic experience in verbal swathings. The hypnotic use of adjectives in the account of Father Dolan's pandying is a small case in point; "hot," "burning," "stinging," "tingling," "crumpled," "flaming," "livid," "scalded," "maimed," "quivering," "fierce," "maddening," all occur in less than half a page. Or again, and more precisely, the story of Wells who shouldered our hero into the square ditch is told on p. 5, retold with more moral commentary (always as an inner monologue) on p. 10, and becomes a fantasy about rats, to be the touch of the prefect's hand, on p. 19. The little boy's feverish round-and-round thinking is represented in this scene by fragments of imagery repeated from previous episodes in the story, by the disintegration of grammar itself, and the loss of logical control to the streaming of imagery:

> The face and the voice went away. Sorry because he was afraid. Afraid that it was some disease. Canker was a disease of plants and cancer one of animals: or another different. That was a long time ago then out on the playgrounds in the evening light, creeping from point to point on the fringe of his line, a heavy bird flying low through the grey light. Leicester Abbey lit up. Wolsey died there. The abbots buried him themselves.

Placed in a new dramatic context, without grammar to control it, the simile which had been perfectly utilitarian and straightforward when used to describe a flying football takes on a new and somber coloring; it is the soul, Wolsey's or Stephen's, moving through mists up and away.

These little details look trifling, but out of them a number of the traits and attitudes of the fledgling artist are shown to emerge. Stephen is a fondler,[3] a collector of words, with which he controls and in effect creates his own universe. He is acutely conscious of names and their emblematic or symbolic import, he is an avid reader of emblems and omens, through which he endeavors to penetrate the veil of circumstance. He tends to find these meanings, or at least to search for them, in moments of fading consciousness, in dreams, trances, and visions; his meditations are not ordered and controlled, as by the *Spiritual Exercises,* they are always tinged with personal emotion, and the truth after which they reach is generally dim and fragmentary.

It is useful to see Stephen developing, on an almost pre-conscious level, the attitudes, not simply of an artist, but of a symbolist poet, because his actual artistic production, in the course of the book, is so scanty and dubious that some critics have thought him the butt of bitter ironic mockery. Indeed, he does very little artistic creating. It is a very literal-minded criticism, though, which insists on being introduced within the artist's workshop so that the authentic pangs of authentic genius can be duly studied and appreciated. We get this sort of thing from the purveyors of popular fiction about tormented titans. Joyce had too much sense and too much good taste to attempt such a display; so, for the most part, he limited his study to the development of those preliminary attitudes and affinities which go into the making of the artist. The creative act itself he left where it belongs— largely out of the picture; this is one more evidence of his basic respect for the artist.

3. one who shows fondness for

# Irony in *A Portrait*

Robert S. Ryf

Robert S. Ryf argues that Joyce uses irony in *A Portrait* in two ways: the Dedalus name and the device of deflation. Ryf cites numerous examples in which Stephen's experiences and proclamations are deflated by an unexpected event, another person, or his own behavior. Irony occurs occasionally, not consistently, Ryf observes, and occurs in connection with Stephen's attitudes, not his ideas. Robert S. Ryf worked for the Columbia Broadcasting System and as a freelance writer before his long career teaching English and comparative literature at Occidental College in Los Angeles. He is the author of *Joseph Conrad*.

Turning to the *Portrait*, we find two principal means by which Joyce sounds overtones of irony: his choice of a name for his hero, and the technique of deflation in its several aspects.

Daedalus is a multi-dimensional name. The accomplishments of this mythical genius were many and varied. In addition to his most noteworthy enterprise—the construction of the labyrinth—he fashioned the golden honeycomb and a hollow wooden cow. The fact is, in the works under consideration, that all these accomplishments are Joyce's: none of them is Stephen's. The labyrinth is not only *Ulysses*, it is the Joyce canon. The golden honeycomb is the labyrinth as a work of art. And in theme and image, there seems to be at least a rough analogy between the hollow wooden cow and Joyce's Ireland.

Stephen is clearly Icarus, not Daedalus. We are given a hint of this at the end of the *Portrait*, when Stephen, preparing for flight, invokes his "father," Daedalus. In *Ulysses*, Stephen directly identifies himself as this fallen son: "Icarus. *Pater, ait.*[1] Seabedabbled, fallen weltering. Lapwing you are." In *Ulysses*, Buck Mulligan hammers home the incon-

1. Father, he was right

Excerpted from *A New Approach to Joyce: The* Portrait of the Artist *as a Guidebook*, by Robert S. Ryf (Berkeley and Los Angeles: University of California Press, 1966).

gruity of Stephen's "absurd name," but in the *Portrait* it is left to the reader to discover the absurdity, although early in the novel our attention is called to the name by a playmate's curiosity about it. "What kind of a name is that?" he asks.

We are reminded of Hamlet's comparison:

My father's brother, but no more like my father
Than I to Hercules: . . .

Hamlet as Hercules is a patent incongruity; Stephen as Daedalus is equally incongruous. What we have then, in effect, is another aspect of the father-son relationship so important to Joyce. Joyce the father (Daedalus) regards from an esthetic distance and with underlying irony the story of Joyce the son (Stephen-Icarus). By using the satire of the incongruous name, Joyce sounds an overtone of irony that reverberates wherever Stephen goes.

### DEFLATION AS A DEVICE

But Joyce does not leave it at this. By tone and technique he expands the dimension of irony in the *Portrait,* and technique prepares us for tone. Deflation is the customary device whereby he injects or reveals the ironic tone. This specialized function of the rhythmic pattern of intermittent pulsations makes its appearance fairly early. In Chapter II, as the young Stephen wants desperately to "meet in the real world the unsubstantial image which his soul so constantly beheld," he imagines this enchanted encounter taking place. "Weakness and timidity and inexperience would fall from him in that magic moment." But two yellow moving vans abruptly intrude and Stephen's house is dismantled. This deflating event confronts Stephen and us with reality, and in retrospect, his vision is revealed as feeble and ludicrous.

There is also an inherent irony in another part of this chapter, when Stephen attempts a poem about Emma Clery:

Now it seemed as if he would fail again but, by dint of brooding on the incident, he thought himself into confidence. During this process all those elements which he deemed common and insignificant fell out of the scene. There remained no trace of the tram itself nor of the trammen nor of the horses: nor did he and she appear vividly. The verses told only of the night and the balmy breeze and the maiden lustre of the moon. Some undefined sorrow was hidden in the hearts of the protagonists as they stood in silence beneath the leafless trees and when the moment of farewell had come the kiss, which had been withheld by one, was given by both. After this the letters L.D.S. were written at the foot of the page and, having hidden the book, he went into his mother's bedroom and gazed at his face for a long time in the mirror of her dressing table.

This would-be poet, who "thinks himself into confidence" to write what sounds like unusually vapid verse, turns out in the end to be a rapt Narcissus.[2]

The ironic tone becomes more overt at the beginning of Chapter IV. Joyce is describing the effects of Stephen's "conversion":

> Every morning he hallowed himself anew in the presence of some holy image or mystery. His day began with an heroic offering of its every moment of thought or action for the intentions of the sovereign pontiff and with an early mass. . . .
>
> His daily life was laid out in devotional areas. By means of ejaculations and prayers he stored up ungrudgingly for the souls in purgatory centuries of days and quarantines and years; yet the spiritual triumph which he felt in achieving with ease so many fabulous ages of canonical penances did not wholly reward his zeal of prayer since he could never know how much temporal punishment he had remitted by way of suffrage for the agonising souls: and, fearful lest in the midst of purgatorial fire, which differed from the infernal only in that it was not everlasting, his penance might avail no more than a drop of moisture he drove his soul daily through an increasing circle of words of supererogation.[3] . . . His life seemed to have drawn near to eternity; every thought, word and deed, every instance of consciousness could be made to revibrate radiantly in heaven: and at times his sense of such immediate repercussion was so lively that he seemed to feel his soul in devotion pressing like fingers the keyboard of a great cash register and to see the amount of his purchase start forth immediately in heaven, not as a number but as a frail column of incense or as a slender flower.

Here, the effect of such ideas as Stephen's neat devotional compartmentation, his heroic ejaculatory mitigation of the plight of multitudes in purgatory, and his dutiful soul driving prepare for the central and inclusive idea—the incense-producing cash register—clearly an image of irony. And his ensuing attempts at self-mortification are infused with satiric overtones that reverberate when Stephen, forcing himself to smell stale odors, says: "I have amended my life, have I not?"

Further deflations await Joyce's hero. The contrapuntal

2. in Greek mythology a youth who pined away in love for his own image in a pool of water and was transformed into a flower    3. going beyond what is required, ordered, or expected

pattern of the scene on the beach has already been mentioned. This juxtaposition of earthbound and unfeeling banter with Stephen's lyric attempt to soar serves as an agent
not only of alienation but of deflation, and Stephen's attitudes are thus made to seem slightly ridiculous in context.
Later, the pronounced deflation that jerks him back from the
contemplation of his vision to the realities of watery tea and
crusts of fried bread serves to orient the entire incident
within a frame of irony.

### LYNCH DEFLATES STEPHEN'S DISCOURSE ON ART

Alienation and deflation go hand in hand most devastatingly
in the scene in which Stephen expounds his esthetic theories
to Lynch. The comments of this irreverent audience of one—
his hangover, Venus' backside, and cowdung—serve as agents
of both alienation and deflation. At every turn, throughout the
discourse his mundane applications of Stephen's theories
serve to point a finger of ridicule at them. Art to Stephen is the
human disposition of sensible or intelligible matter for an esthetic end. But the only esthetic end desired by Lynch is a job
paying five hundred a year. Stephen illustrates one of his
points by reference to the hypothenuse of a right-angled tri-
angle, but Lynch prefers the hypothenuse of the Venus of
Praxiteles.[4] Stephen tries to illustrate another point, and
searches for an example:

"—Let us take woman—said Stephen.

"—Let us take her!—said Lynch fervently." But Lynch is
not the only agent of deflation: "A long dray laden with old
iron came round the corner of Sir Patrick Dun's hospital cov-
ering the end of Stephen's speech with the harsh roar of jan-
gled and rattling metal." Stephen persists, however. He postu-
lates his three qualities of the esthetic object and wins mock
applause from Lynch: "—Bull's eye again!—said Lynch wit-
tily. Tell me now what is claritas and you win the cigar.—"
Stephen does so, enamored of his theories: "Stephen paused
and, though his companion did not speak, felt that his words
had called up around them a thought enchanted silence." But
the enchantment of silence fades when Stephen tries out his
esthetic catechism on Lynch:

> —*If a man hacking in fury at a block of wood*—Stephen con-
> tinued—*make there an image of a cow, is that image a work*

4. a 4th Century BC Greek sculptor

## JOYCE'S IRONIC BALANCING ACT

*Patrick Parrinder calls* A Portrait *an "ironic autobiography"; he says the irony occurs as Joyce balances the possible points of view the reader might take toward Stephen.*

It sets out to be an impersonal or ironic autobiography. The irony consists in Joyce's balancing of the different points of view it is possible to adopt towards the young Stephen. Stephen himself comes to believe he is following a predestined course, and unfolds a fervently idealistic artistic creed. Through him Joyce is able both to affirm the romantic myth of artistic genius, and to partially dissociate himself from the arrogance and self-conceit which follows from that myth. Irony is always implicit in the narrative, yet it cannot be too heavily underlined or it will destroy the basis of Joyce's—not merely Stephen's—claims for his writing. The book is uncertainly poised between mature reservation and an almost intoxicating sympathy with Stephen's experience. Finally, it may be, the artist-myth in the *Portrait* taken on its own was too powerful, and Joyce's attempt to relive it burst the bounds of mature detachment. He then had to create a disillusioned sequel to his autobiographical novel, in the parts of *Ulysses* centred on Stephen.

Patrick Parrinder, "Joyce's *Portrait* and the Proof of the Oracle," in Harold Bloom, ed., *James Joyce's* A Portrait of the Artist as a Young Man. New York: Chelsea House, 1988.

*of art? If not, why not?*

—That's a lovely one—said Lynch, laughing again.—That has the true scholastic stink.—

Stephen now reaches the climax of his discourse, and approaches what may be his key doctrine—that of the impersonality of the artist: "The artist, like the God of the creation, remains within or behind or beyond or above his handiwork, invisible, refined out of existence, indifferent, paring his fingernails." But his companion, true to form, counters with this *reductio ad absurdum*:[5] "—Trying to refine them also out of existence—said Lynch." Rain begins to fall, and the two seek shelter. And with the rain comes the final deflation: "—What do you mean—Lynch asked surlily—by prating about beauty and the imagination in this miserable God forsaken island? No wonder the artist retired within or behind his handiwork after having perpetrated this coun-

5. disproof of a proposition by showing the absurdity of its inevitable conclusion

try.—" This final observation, which effectively throws cold water on all Stephen's discourse, ends the scene. Stephen's theories have been buffeted by Lynch, epitomizing external reality, and, thus buffeted, emerge into the open air having lost some of the glitter that was theirs while safely ensconced in the cloister of Stephen's mind.

If Stephen's esthetic theory is treated at least part ironically, so is his artistic production. The process of composition of the villanelle is described lyrically enough, but the context is onanistic;[6] the framework of the scene is thus one of irony.

## THE FINAL DEFLATION AND IRONY

A further deflation, one of the most powerful in the *Portrait*, awaits Stephen in the final chapter, as he drifts into erotic reverie

> It was not thought nor vision, though he knew vaguely that her figure was passing homeward through the city. Vaguely first and then more sharply he smelt her body. A conscious unrest seethed in his blood. Yes, it was her body he smelt: a wild and languid smell: the tepid limbs over which his music had flowed desirously and the secret soft linen upon which her flesh distilled odour and a dew.
>
> A louse crawled over the nape of his neck and, putting his thumb and forefinger deftly beneath his loose collar, he caught it.

If the flesh of his beloved distills "odour and a dew," Stephen's flesh distills a louse. This abrupt and jarring juxtaposition effectively deflates his throbbing vision.

In the diary entries that constitute the final section of the *Portrait* we find Stephen posing as martyr "Crossing Stephen's, that is, my green . . ." This self-identification with the historical martyr[7] gives us another of Joyce's controlled glimpses of Stephen; by the use of this association, Joyce gives us a carefully balanced view in which judgment and sympathy go hand in hand. There is considerable truth in Stephen's equation of alienation with martyrdom, and there is also more than a grain of irony.

This brings us to the ending of the *Portrait*, and to Stephen's proclamation: "Welcome, O life! I go to encounter for the millionth time the reality of experience and to forge in the smithy of my soul the uncreated conscience of my

6. related to masturbation   7. Stephen, the New Testament martyr, stoned for blasphemy

race." Stephen is completely serious in making this statement, but I suggest that our reaction to it becomes inevitably
a mixed one and that there are several reasons for this.

First, we are aware that this is quite a heroic attitude Stephen
is striking here, and in retrospect we cannot avoid sensing that
Joyce's tone is slightly ironic. Stephen is going to encounter
"for the millionth time the reality of experience," but we are
aware that his encounters with the reality of experience in the
past have usually led to his rejection of that reality.

Stephen in essence is playing God, and will forge the "uncreated conscience" of his race. Whether we interpret the
word "conscience" as having to do with morality or whether
we are mindful of its derivation from a word meaning "consciousness"—and readers of Joyce become aware that most
of his key words are used in more than one sense—the implication is the same. Stephen is here postulating himself as
supreme creator.

But the key word in the entire passage, it seems to me, is
the verb "forge." One meaning is explicit: to create. . . .

The idea of Stephen as forger should not surprise us. His
pitifully few attempts at artistic creation in the *Portrait* are
narcissistic or onanistic forgeries. Whether out of bitterness
or because of a desire to reveal and emphasize, Joyce gives
us a portrait of Shem[8] as a caricature of Stephen. This later
glimpse confirms or exposes the generally overlooked ironic
implications of the ending of the *Portrait. Ulysses* is the in-
termediate step. "Signatures of all things I am here to read,"
meditates Stephen in the Proteus episode. But an artist is
here neither to read signatures nor to forge them, but to
originate them.

## THE DRAMATIC IRONY OF THE ENDING

Thus, the irony of the ending of the *Portrait* is dramatic
irony. Stephen intends one meaning, but we are conscious
not only of his meaning but of another. We view him as a
youth assuming a mission for which he is not yet qualified.

I have not intended to imply that the *Portrait* is out and
out satire: it is not. "Irony" is the more accurate word, and
irony is only one of the several aspects or dimensions of this
novel. Joyce's ironic tone is not constantly present; it is used
occasionally, but always with telling effect. When present, it

8. a character in Joyce's *Finnegans Wake*

constitutes a surrounding aura through which we view Stephen. And this aura, ironically, does not obscure him—it reveals him. It is most overtly in evidence in connection with two aspects of Stephen's life: his temporary conversion, and his attitudes toward art and the artist. And here, I think, we arrive at a distinction. It is not Stephen's actions that are customarily viewed ironically, it is his attitudes. When he is deflated, it is by his own terms, and the deflations come when his attitudes are confronted by external realities.

I am aware that to establish the presence of irony in the *Portrait* is to raise serious questions, and here I must deal with the second of the opposing critical stances mentioned at the beginning of this chapter. If Stephen is an object of irony, can he be taken seriously as a vehicle for the criticism of those aspects of Ireland seemingly under fire in Joyce's novel? And what of Stephen's aspiration to "forge . . . the uncreated conscience" of his race—is Joyce ridiculing this aspiration? Is he sneering at the moral purpose seemingly implied in the statement? I believe that the answer to the first question is yes, to the others, no.

Several observations may be made here, the combined import of which supplies these answers. In the first place, we must always remember Joyce's distinction between proper and improper art. Proper art is above and beyond desire or loathing; it is subject matter for contemplation. In writing the *Portrait*, Joyce was not writing a tract. He was directing his novel at readers of mature imagination, capable of absorbing the multidimensional meaning of the structure, of which irony is one dimension.

Second, much of the irony in the novel manifests itself in the repeated clashes between Stephen's artistic imagination and the world of external reality. Surely the implication here is that the world in which Stephen finds himself submerged—the world he is trying to escape—is no fertile breeding ground for art or creative endeavor. Thus the "criticism" of Church and country to be found in the *Portrait*—mainly in the form of suggestion, image, rhythm, and tone—can, I think, be taken seriously.

## THE IRONY OF STEPHEN'S ATTITUDES

To repeat an earlier observation, it is Stephen's attitudes that are presented ironically, rather than the ideas he is promulgating. We have seen that his ideas on art and esthetic theory were certainly taken seriously by Joyce, who constructed his works upon them. But here is Stephen glibly announcing dogma. The natural question is: Why is he not creating instead of codifying? The few scraps of verse we may credit him with in the course of the *Portrait* hardly qualify him as an authority. He seems more concerned with himself and his self-announced mission at the moment than he does with real creativity.

We arrive now at the question of the "uncreated conscience." The irony here is not directed at the idea itself but at the fact that Stephen is as yet in no position to forge it except in the pejorative sense. We must remind ourselves again of the esthetic distance separating Joyce from Stephen. As is clearly evident from reading his works, Joyce passed through and emerged from the "Stephen" phase and, by the very writing of his works, forged the uncreated conscience of his race. No writer who was so keenly aware of spiritual hungers, who so consistently wrote against sham, pretense, hypocrisy, insensitivity, and unthinking conformity, who upheld integrity and honesty was, to say the very least, insensitive to moral considerations. We may quite safely conclude, I think, that the forging of the uncreated conscience was a legitimate and vital mission to Joyce, and one not to be ridiculed. And if there is irony in Stephen's announcement, it is the irony of a young esthete who, before he is qualified to undertake such a task, has much yet to learn and does not realize it.

Finally, it is helpful to remember, at the risk of reiteration, that irony is not everywhere and at all times present in the novel. I have described many of Joyce's techniques and rhythms as being patterns of interrupted or intermittent pulsations, and his tone in the *Portrait*, I think, constitutes another such pattern. Joyce coins a word in *Ulysses* which seems to fit here. That word is "jocoserious." As we consider the *Portrait*, with its fluctuations of tone pattern, we realize that it is a "jocoserious" novel. Realizing this, we are in a position to see that the comic spirit in Joyce's later writings, now generally recognized, did not originate in a vacuum, and that the seeds of it can be seen in the *Portrait*.

# CHAPTER 6

# Critical Evaluation of *A Portrait*

# *A Portrait* at Fifty

William T. Noon

Fifty years after *A Portrait's* 1916 publication, William T. Noon assesses the volume of critical attention the novel has generated and its popularity with readers. Noon summarizes Stephen's qualities and the book's unique structure, which engage readers. Reflecting on the adolescent nature of Stephen and the literary and historical context in which Joyce wrote *A Portrait*, Noon concludes that Stephen's story will probably not become outdated. William T. Noon taught English at Le Moyne College in Syracuse, New York. Besides writing numerous articles on Joyce for scholarly journals, he is the author of *Joyce and Aquinas* and *Poetry and Prayer.*

*A Portrait of the Artist as a Young Man* was first published from London in the *Egoist* magazine. [American poet] Ezra Pound sponsored its publication and transmitted installments of about fifteen pages each to the editor. It ran serially, with a few breaks, from February 2, 1914, James Joyce's thirty-second birthday, until September 1, 1915. Substantially the same text was used when it was first published in book form December 29, 1916, by B.W. Huebsch, New York. . . .

## *A PORTRAIT* GENERATES NUMEROUS STUDIES

*A Portrait* is today a literary classic, widely read, much commented on, often reprinted. I do not know the statistics of publication for all of Joyce's works, but I expect that *A Portrait* is the one most widely read. All bibliographies of scholarly studies in literature include items about this book in ever-accelerating frequency: *PMLA, Review of English Studies, Modern Fiction Studies, Abstracts of English Studies, Cambridge Bibliography of English Literature, Modern Language Review, International Index,* and so forth. The *James Joyce Quarterly* (which began publication in 1963) now of-

Excerpted from "*A Portrait of the Artist as a Young Man:* After Fifty Years," by William T. Noon, in *James Joyce Today: Essays on Major Works,* edited by Thomas F. Staley. Copyright ©1966 by Indiana University Press. Reprinted with permission from Indiana University Press.

ten carries an extended "Supplemental JJ Checklist" by Alan
M. Cohn,[1] sometimes with Richard M. Kain. *The James Joyce
Review* (discontinued in 1959) used formerly to carry with
some regularity entries in "James Joyce Studies" by William
White. All these lists include innumerable items about *A
Portrait*. So does Robert H. Deming's *A Bibliography of
James Joyce Studies*, No. 18 in the Library Series of the Uni-
versity of Kansas Publications, 1964. The Special Number
"James Joyce" of *Modern Fiction Studies*, way back (so it
now seems) in 1958, carried a long selected checklist by
Maurice Beebe and Walton Litz of special studies of Joyce's
separate works. This highly selective, partial list includes
nearly two finely printed pages of recommended titles on *A
Portrait*. There has been no dearth in the making of books
and articles about *A Portrait*, and there is no end in view.
Here now comes another!

Some of these articles and books are stimulated artifi-
cially, to be sure, as it were from on high, by Joyce's
present-day towering position in the Academy, or "Estab-
lishment" (as that Academy is often referred to and refers to
itself). How Joyce might have smiled! Some of this artificial
stimulation is forced or fostered by the hothouse environment of certain schools, colleges, graduate departments,
where Joyce's works are highly privileged touchstones of a
literary student's or a professor's competence. Joycean ex-
pertise is a well-known trademark of scholarly industry. It
tends to become an industry all by itself, establishing its
own monopoly of experts. It looks at times as though it
might become a swindle. . . .

### *A PORTRAIT*'S APPEAL FOR READERS

But the prestige-symbol value of *A Portrait* does not explain
its whole story. This book must have something vital still to
say to modern minds and imaginations, and Joyce must here
still say it in an arresting way, if one is to account for this book
of his being so much written about, possibly over-written
about today. Why is Joyce "in" when so many of his peers are
now "out"? Literary fads come and go. But Joyce goes on. . . .
In spite of Establishments and Academies, a book or author
cannot for over fifty years hold literary stature as a classic
against the will of the people who read. Young people, in par-

---

1. The names identified in this survey of lists of Joyce studies are scholars and critics.

ticular—all, at their best, experimentalists—know what they like and value, and they are not inarticulate in letting their seniors know what values and likes they intend to make prevail. They are coming up all the time into the "Establishments." And at this most outspoken moment, 1966, and after fifty years, Joyce's *A Portrait* is still a widely prevailing book. . . .

Now, as already suggested, in 1966 the big questions that one needs to ask about Joyce's *A Portrait of the Artist as a Young Man* are: Does this story still come through? Is it an important novel of spiritual growth? Of artistic and intellectual rebellion? Or is it a period piece? Has it been overread, overstudied? Is it outdated in its exotic concerns? Readers sometimes admire that which they do not like.

No one claims for *A Portrait* the same quality of classic, enduring excellence that belongs unassailably to *Ulysses*. Nor might the usual reader who admires *A Portrait* and who has backed away from *Finnegans Wake* claim that Joyce's first novel has the even-now daring importance of his last major work. Is *A Portrait,* indeed, worth the close attention that most readers gladly give to Joyce's earlier *Dubliners* short stories?

I judge from my own experience with young readers, women and men, seminarians some, that for most *A Portrait* still speaks to them and is a story that most of them both admire and like. *A Portrait* shows movement, inside and outside the mind. It is not grounded as is the *Stephen Hero* fragment. Although Stephen in both versions follows a solitary path to his art, there is a note of artistic inevitability sounded in *A Portrait* that is not heard in the fragment. In both versions Stephen makes choices. But in the fragment one feels that although Stephen's life in Ireland was so lackluster he could have acted differently, whereas in *A Portrait* one feels that since his life in Ireland was this way Stephen had no other choice.

Most readers of A *Portrait* conclude that Stephen Dedalus is egocentric. At times he comes through as a kind of over-intellectualized pedant, as an esthete rather than as an artist. Or if an artist, at times he appears to be immature, a too easily wounded young man, like Richard Rowan in Joyce's play, *Exiles.* Richard, one feels, tries too hard to break all bonds, divine and human, including those of love. So one senses that his weary isolation at the end is owing to his own limitations. His "deep, deep wound of doubt" tires spectators just as much as it tires Richard.

Stephen Dedalus is also an intelligently sensitive young man. He is supremely dedicated to his art. Only at the end of the story does he feel obligated to withdraw from his society. He concludes at the start, however, that it is a too much settled, sick society. He concludes at the end that it can only paralyze all his artistic energies by those pressures that others have since come to call mass-cult and mass-mediocrity. His is a story of the loss of faith; it is also a story of the search for faith. And how might any story both of the loss of faith and the search for faith grow irrelevant in the twentieth century?

Stephen is searching for the good life: he wants to be whole. He hopes to be just. He is determined to be himself. *A Portrait* is certainly more than just a diatribe against turn-of-the-century Dublin society. As the title itself phrases it, this is the story of an *artist as a young man*. It is more than just a planned program of aesthetic rebellion and reform. Stephen is mixed-up, sometimes too readily injured or hurt. At the end, and in spite of his rhetoric, he realizes that he cannot replace God through the creative processes of literature, much as he might like to. Such, anyway, is Joyce's more mature point in this novel. At the end of *A Portrait*, Stephen pledges himself "to forge in the smithy of my soul the uncreated conscience of my race." Even in this moment of withdrawal from Dublin, he is not forever renouncing all links. He has resolved to be more than just an Outsider, even as he goes away. He badly wants always to love the city that he is leaving behind. He remembers and recalls his mother's words to him as she packed his "new secondhand clothes" for his journey: "She prays now, she says, that I may learn in my own life and away from home and friends what the heart is and what it feels. Amen. So be it."

### THE STORY IN FIVE STAGES

The story of *A Portrait* unfolds symmetrically in five stages of Stephen Dedalus' spiritual development. The inner chapters, II, III, and IV, are mostly about his days in Belvedere College, a Jesuit high school for boys in the heart of Dublin. The first chapter is mostly about Stephen's experiences as a child, his first days in school at the then rather exclusive Jesuit boarding-school for boys, Clongowes Wood College, in County Kildare, not far from Dublin. The last chapter, V, the longest, is mostly about Stephen's college days at University

College, also in Dublin, and at that time also conducted by the Jesuits. There are brief interludes elsewhere. In the first chapter there is one interlude that describes Stephen's troubled visit home to Dublin for Christmas; it presents the sad-glad Christmas dinner where sharp controversy about the fall of Charles Stewart Parnell bewilders young Stephen and extinguishes everyone's Christmas spirits. In the second chapter there are interludes that describe Stephen's holiday visits to Blackrock on the sea, and to Cork. These are both places where Joyce briefly lived with his family when he himself was a boy.

For each of these five chapters there is a more-or-less dominant image (or symbol), a rather pervasive emotion recollected, and at the end a rather marked pause, a stasis in the action of the story. As each chapter concludes, there is for Stephen a special, new kind of going away.

In Chapter I, the dominant image is Father Dolan's pandy-bat; the dominant emotion, a fear of grown-ups; and the pause of recollection, a sense of grateful relief at Father Arnall's taking his part. So it is as Stephen leaves childhood. In Chapter II, "a breakwater of order and elegance against the sordid tide of life without him" variously serves as image; the guilt of the model schoolboy is the pervasive emotion (for already Stephen begins to doubt his religious faith); and "the swoon of sin" in the brothel is the moment of stasis at the end. So he forsakes innocence and the life of sanctifying grace. In Chapter III, shortest of the chapters, Father Arnall's terrifying retreat-sermons on the punishment of the damned in hell—"fetid carcasses," "pain of intensity"—provide an image that is truly dominant; Stephen's emotion here is one of supernatural fright; the pause of recollection at the end describes Stephen's receiving the Holy Eucharist after he has made his retreat-confession. For the time being, at least, he goes away from a life of sin. In Chapter IV, there occurs what is probably the dominant image of the whole book, Stephen's vision (part sight, part imagination) of the young wading girl in the stream; the dominant emotion is that of profane joy for the "hawklike man" in his recognition of his true vocation, to be not a priest at the altar but a priest of the eternal imagination; here the stasis at the end describes Stephen's walk in the moonlight beside the sea. He knows that he has said "no" to his priestly calling: "On and on and on and on!". In the concluding Chapter V, the dominant im-

age is that of swallows (wild geese) in flight; the pervasive
emotion, loneliness; the final stasis is Stephen's silent moment of poise just before flight. As absolutely as he may, he
is about to go away from home.

## *A PORTRAIT* IN CONTRAST

*A Portrait* has, of course, literary antecedents. There is much
uncertainty here, because Joyce was too much his own man
for a commentator to state categorically just what these ar-
chetypes of the author might have been. The novel of spiritual
development and of adolescent revolt is one that goes back at
least as far as [British novelist] Samuel Butler's *The Way of All
Flesh* (not published until 1903) and the various confessions
of [Anglo-Irish novelist and playwright] George Moore. It has
roots in the French symbolists, and also in [British writer]
John Addington Symonds' many French-oriented volumes on
the artists of the Renaissance and of Romanticism. In Germany, it has even earlier forebears in [poet and playwright
Johann Wolfgang von] Goethe's *Werther* (1774, 1787) and
*Dichtung und Wahrheit* (1831). This tradition includes, of
course, and for Joyce especially, [British writer John Henry]
Newman's *Apologia* (1864) and, to be sure, Saint Augustine's
*Confessions* (c. 400). There is already evidence available that
Joyce had read all these books, or at least looked into them.
How well in scholarly detail he might have known them is ar-
guable. He probably read them hurriedly, as most artists are
wont to read others' books. But he knew what was in the air!
He had his own story to tell, and he ended up telling it in his
own way. He had sense enough (in his mind, maybe not in
his heart) to know that no artist's new way of telling a story
ever catches on with others at once. There is always a time-
lag. Modern minds are not nearly so modern as non-artists
often imagine. With *A Portrait*, Joyce took his own risks.

As one looks back now on this story, it appears to be as
much an elegy for a lost cause as it does a manifesto for the
cause that its young man, an artist, proclaimed he would
bring into being. *Forge* as a writer might by fabricating or
counterfeiting, no artist *creates* consciences, certainly not for
his entire race. God alone creates *ex nihilo sui et subjecti.*[2]
Men at their best can only hope to transform or modify. No
young man can create a brand new world to suit his own

2. by bringing forth out of nothingness

tastes and specifications. God himself respects other persons' individual freedom of choice. Ireland (or Dublin) is now much different from what it was fifty years ago. Now, for example, it is proud to boast of James Joyce as a Dubliner, but its conscience is far from being the one that Stephen Dedalus promised to forge. By the time, indeed, that Joyce drew his final *Portrait* of Stephen Dedalus, he himself abroad had come to accept the situation in Dublin and all the human beings caught up in it with a wryly amused compassion. After all, 1916 was the year of the Easter Uprising,[3] a Dublin happening that "transformed utterly" the comedy of life for all Dubliners, not just for [poet] W.B. Yeats. Francis Sheehey-Skeffington, Joyce's old friend of the University College days, was shot on the second day of that insurrection. In this story, *A Portrait,* already written before the Rising, Stephen may no longer think of himself as hero, but he still likes to play the role of pure and passive martyr: Stephen martyr, *Bous Stephanoumenos, Bous Stephaneferos.* He likes to think of himself as the sacrificial ox, the scapegoat, who bears his people's guilt but who also bears the poet's crown. Simon Dedalus is not the only one who is weeping for Parnell,[4] his "uncrowned king," when the famous Christmas dinner scene in the first chapter of this novel comes to a close. So is Stephen! So are most readers. So, one supposes, was Joyce when he composed the scene. One also supposes that he smiled. *Lacrimae rerum:* the tears of things, and their absurdity too.

Joyce did not need in 1916 to look back so far through the haze at Stephen as we need to. Stephen is not altogether admirable, nor are any of these other Dubliners. With infinite pains Joyce tells their story well. It is mostly a tale of adolescent disillusionment. It is about the artistic aspiration of a young man to be self-possessed, self-achieving, self-aware. Stephen would like to be accepted by the world to which he belongs. This is usual enough. It is the kind of story that will probably never go out of date.

---

3. an armed nationalist insurrection in Dublin; many were killed, arrested and deported   4. Charles Stewart Parnell was a member of Parliament who supported Home Rule. He died in 1891.

# *A Portrait* Breaks the Mold

John Blades

John Blades argues that *A Portrait* makes a significant contribution to the modernist movement in literature. In comparison with *Stephen Hero*, Joyce's first rendition of Stephen's story, Blade highlights *A Portrait's* modern features. He identifies several of Joyce's innovative techniques, such as a silent narrator, epiphanies, and the stream-of-consciousness method. The weaknesses of the novel, Blade says, lie with the character of Stephen. John Blades lectures in English at Cleveland College, Redcar, U.K., where he is researching the works of James Joyce.

It is a curious thing that during Joyce's lifetime *A Portrait* received a generally warmer reception among poets than among novelists—[William Butler] Yeats, [Ezra] Pound and Hart Crane are among those who found it an inspiring novel, perhaps because they found an affinity of poetic spirit in the struggles of its hero. However, the wider response to the novel has inevitably been affected, usually adversely, by comparisons with *Ulysses*, which appeared six years after *A Portrait*. The success of *Ulysses* has also tended to divert attention away from *A Portrait* as critics have preferred to concentrate on the former, justly regarded as Joyce's mature triumph and a novel which has had an enormous influence on twentieth-century literature and thinking.

## *A PORTRAIT* ADVANCES THE NOVEL BEYOND *STEPHEN HERO*

However, *A Portrait* is a landmark in the progress of the novel, both in terms of its anticipation of the techniques of *Ulysses* and *Finnegans Wake,* and in its own right; a useful starting point in evaluating it as such a landmark is to compare it with Joyce's earlier draft for the novel, *Stephen Hero.*

Excerpted from *James Joyce:* A Portrait of the Artist as a Young Man, by John Blades. Copyright ©1991 by John Blades. Reprinted with permission from Penguin Books, Ltd., UK.

Whereas *A Portrait* is unequivocally a novel of this century, especially for its techniques, *Stephen Hero* is fixed firmly in the tradition of the nineteenth-century novel. The narrator is persistently intrusive and frequently intervenes by directly addressing the reader, to comment on the action and on Stephen. In addition, there are long passages of explicit description or comment; conversations are laboured though realistic; epiphanies have become diluted in their effect rather than being, as they are in *A Portrait,* tight and succinct. In general terms, the considerable explicit discussion in *Stephen Hero* of themes and the detailed explanation of attitudes and motives render the total effect ponderous.

One of the clearest differences between the two versions can be seen in the relative silence of the narrator in *A Portrait.* As we have discovered, material is presented more baldly and with greater discipline and economy, and the reader's imagination is aroused to fill the gaps; where *Stephen Hero* attempts to formulate or define, *A Portrait* instead seeks to communicate the actual intensity of experience itself, forcefully inviting the reader to share in it. But a further point which strikes the reader in comparing the two is that in *A Portrait* Stephen's artistic development is made its central theme; everything in the novel—characters, themes, techniques and point of view—is focused through it, unifying all the diverse elements of the novel.

There are fundamental differences between the two versions in the presentation of character—in *A Portrait* we see almost nothing of Stephen's brothers and sisters. In the earlier version his brother, Maurice, prominently fulfils the parts of confidant, confessor, and adviser (occupying the equivalent place in Stephen's life as Stanislaus in Joyce's); he is mentioned only once by name in *A Portrait* as a 'thick-headed ruffian.' There is also more direct criticism of Mr Dedalus in *Stephen Hero* as the cause of the family's suffering, while Mrs Dedalus is shown as more vitally sympathetic to Stephen. In this respect she resembles Mrs Morel, mother of the artist in [D.H.] Lawrence's *Sons and Lovers,* trying to share her son's interests and appearing at least open-minded, if not actually encouraging, to his radical ideas (up to a point at least.) However, in *A Portrait,* unlike the mothers in either *Stephen Hero* or *Sons and Lovers,* Mrs Dedalus is realized only incompletely; her suffering is barely hinted at and she appears to exist, like so many of the other characters, simply as a foil to Stephen's character.

Comparing the two versions, the overall effect of these changes in Stephen's relationships is a marked intensification in his isolation. In *Stephen Hero,* Stephen's isolation comes about as a result of his ideas and the hostility of those around him, making him appear to a large extent a victim of his situation, whereas in *A Portrait* his isolation is of his own making, the result of his own withdrawal, a deliberate policy of self-exile making him cold and lacking in human feeling.

## JOYCE'S TECHNICAL INNOVATIONS

On the other hand, it is principally Joyce's technical innovations which stamp the novel as a great leap forward and which established both it and Joyce in the foreground of the Modernist movement. The way of Stephen's mind was something new in literature and the free approach of Joyce's presentation reflects this apparent emancipation. As we have seen, one of the chief among the novel's innovations is the modulation of styles to parallel and reinforce changes in Stephen's life, continually varying the distances and relationships between narrator and character and reader to facilitate both comment and humour, creating a dynamic flux of surfaces and tensions. In this way Joyce essentially fuses together his subject matter and its form, components traditionally treated in isolation, with Stephen Dedalus thus becoming the total experience of the novel (an approach which prepares us for that in *Ulysses* with its even more radical experiments in style and language).

We have seen how the need for such modulation arises, partly as a result of Joyce's avowed approach of employing a *silent* narrator to exclude all direct authorial intrusion into the novel for direct comment. To retain control, Joyce is prompted into adopting a range of alternative techniques. By far the most effective of these is the use of the dual consciousness—Stephen's and the narrator's—to retain the intimacy of the first-person form of narration while at the same time allowing some degree of comment by way of the mature perspective of the narrator. The stream-of-consciousness method of presenting Stephen's development, together with Joyce's unique use of epiphanies for disposing the story, brilliantly cultivates the novel's structure, issuing organically from within the consciousness of the novel's hero rather than being imposed from outside by an explicit narrator.

These are techniques which find their full maturity in *Ulysses* though there is no sense in which *A Portrait* is less accomplished in what it sets out to achieve. Indeed, in comparing *A Portrait* and *Ulysses*, the earlier novel usually appears less rigorously organized by its techniques which are less foregrounded, making it also appear lyrical and naturalistic. However, it is through comparison with the rich universe of *Ulysses* that the weaknesses of *A Portrait* also become most apparent.

## THE LIMITATIONS OF STEPHEN

Essentially, the problems of the novel are the problems of its central figure. Next to *Ulysses* and even to *Dubliners, A Portrait* comes through as a sombre, earnest production but lacking most in humour and almost completely in human warmth, a direct consequence of the manifest limitations of its main character. There is none of the vigorous wit and philosophical irony of the genial *Dubliners* and of *Ulysses*, while Joyce's own waggish satire is only hinted at—for instance, in the visit to Cork, and briefly in the Christmas dinner scene.

Another source of dissatisfaction with *A Portrait* is, ironically, the novel's point of view and the consciousness itself of its central character. We have already considered how the strict discipline of the novel's viewpoint through Stephen's eyes helps to create intimacy and at the same time to emphasize his solitude. Yet it also engineers an intense claustrophobia which in Chapter 3 helps to consolidate the themes of guilt and entrapment, but by Chapter 5 becomes oppressive and wearying. More important is the effect of Stephen's own limitations on that viewpoint. One of the novel's chief drawbacks is the character of Stephen himself, especially aspects like his callous pride, lack of humanity and obsessively dogmatic attitude to life. These inevitably contribute to the narrowness of the novel's vision—not only do we see a shrinking of his capacity and willingness to embrace life, but we also see this brought about through the flawed mentality of Stephen. Joyce himself, when considering a central character for *Ulysses*, dismissed the possibility of using Stephen, describing him as an 'immature persona,' having a shape that cannot easily be changed, after it appears to be hardened in that posture at the end of *A Portrait*. Because of these limitations, Stephen is unable to reflect

---

**STREAM-OF-CONSCIOUSNESS DEFINED**

*A. Nicholas Fargnoli and Michael Patrick Gillespie define stream-of-consciousness and explain how it is similar to and different from interior monologue.*

**stream of consciousness** A phrase coined by [American philosopher] William James in his *Principles of Psychology* (1890) to describe the flow of ideas, perceptions, sensations and recollections that characterize human thought. It has subsequently been adopted by literary critics and authors to describe the representation of this flow in writing.

Although it is very similar to and often confused with interior monologue, stream of consciousness is characterized by markedly distinct technical features. The reason for the confusion is that, as in interior monologue, stream of consciousness jumps rapidly from topic to topic with little regard for logical progression or coherent transitions. However, unlike interior monologue, stream-of-consciousness writing is governed by basic rules of grammar and syntax. Although many critics associate Joyce with the stream-of-consciousness technique, it would be more accurate to identify Joyce's efforts as interior monologue.

A. Nicholas Fargnoli and Michael Patrick Gillespie, *James Joyce A to Z: The Essential Reference to the Life and Work.* New York: Oxford University Press, 1995.

---

positively—as we see him begin to do in the 'Proteus' chapter of *Ulysses*—except in terms of arrogance and egoism. Consequently, there is no genuine sense of sustained inner conflict and thus neither the creative tension nor the humanity which would otherwise have been generated. Any possibility of true self-realization within the range of the novel is excluded, and it concludes unsympathetically with Stephen not so much blind as wilful. While the need for self-realization is highlighted in the closing pages with the insistence of Cranly and Mrs Dedalus on the requirement for ordinary humanity, Stephen himself coldly records on the final page:

> She prays now, she says, that I may learn in my own life and away from home and friends what the heart is and what it feels. Amen.

But it is not treated seriously by Stephen until the early chapters of *Ulysses*, and is not made real until his momentous encounter with Leopold Bloom in that novel.

Just as Joyce's relationship with Stephen Dedalus is something new in the novel, so the novel itself was never the same again after *A Portrait;* its enduring significance is as a major landmark in the development of Modernism, issuing principally from the crisis of confidence in the efficacy of the word. It is typified here in the instability of the text and of the moral stances; the undermining of established author-reader relationships, and their replacement with confrontational authorial silences; the primacy of myth and the new psychological realities, expressed through archetype, symbol, epiphany, and the stream of consciousness. If Stephen's closing words express the anxiety and doubt for his future, they also perfectly express the same doubt and uncertainty of the Modernist predicament. This is the achievement of *A Portrait*; the trick, as someone said, is living with it.

# CHRONOLOGY

**1882**

James Joyce born February 2; Henrik Ibsen publishes *An Enemy of the People.*

**1888**

Joyce enters Clongowes Wood College in September.

**1890**

Ibsen publishes *Hedda Gabler;* first moving pictures shown in New York City.

**1891**

Joyce withdrawn from Clongowes Wood College.

**1893**

Joyce family moves to Dublin; Joyce enters Belvedere College; Henry Ford builds first American automobile.

**1898**

Joyce graduates from Belvedere College, enrolls in University College, Dublin.

**1899**

Ibsen publishes *When We Dead Awaken;* Irish Literary Theater founded.

**1900**

Joyce's review, "Ibsen's New Drama," appears in *Fortnightly Review,* April 1.

**1901**

Joyce publishes "The Day of the Rabblement," essay attacking Irish Literary Theater; first Nobel Prizes awarded.

**1902**

Joyce graduates from University College, Dublin, with degree in modern languages; leaves for Paris.

**1903**

Joyce's mother dies; Joyce returns to Ireland; Wright brothers' first flight.

**1904**

Joyce meets Nora Barnacle June 10; falls in love with her June 16; Joyce and Nora leave for Europe in October, settle in Pola, Italy.

**1905**

Joyce and Nora settle in Trieste; son, George (Georgio), born July 27; Joyce's brother Stanislaus moves to Trieste; Albert Einstein publishes first theory of relativity.

**1906**

Joyce, Nora, and Georgio move to Rome; Ibsen dies.

**1907**

Joyce, Nora and Georgio return to Trieste; *Chamber Music* published; daughter, Lucia, born July 26; Pablo Picasso paints *Les Demoiselles d'Avignon;* first Cubist exhibition in Paris.

**1909**

Joyce visits Ireland twice; second time opens Volta cinema in Dublin.

**1912**

Joyce makes his last trip to Ireland with his family.

**1913**

Ezra Pound contacts Joyce, in whom he recognizes literary talent.

**1914**

*A Portrait of the Artist as a Young Man* serialized in the *Egoist* through 1915; *Dubliners* published; Joyce begins *Ulysses.*

**1915**

Joyce moves to Zurich, Switzerland; *Exiles* and *A Portrait of the Artist as a Young Man* are complete.

**1916**

Joyce publishes *A Portrait of the Artist as a Young Man.*

**1918**

*Ulysses* begins serialization in the *Little Review* through 1920; *Exiles* published.

**1919**

Five installments of *Ulysses* serialized in the *Egoist;* first stage production of *Exiles* in German; Joyce, Nora, Georgio, and Lucia return to Trieste in October.

**1920**

Joyce and family move to Paris in July; the *Little Review* ordered to cease publishing installments of *Ulysses.*

**1922**

*Ulysses* published by Shakespeare and Company, Paris; U.S. Post Office destroys copies on arrival; Ireland partitioned.

**1923**

Joyce begins *Finnegans Wake.*

**1924**

First fragments of *Work in Progress* appear in *transatlantic review;* Adolf Hitler publishes *Mein Kampf.*

**1926**

*Ulysses* pirated and published serially in *Two Worlds Monthly* through 1927; Stalin rises to power in Russia.

**1927**

Joyce's *Work in Progress* begins to appear in regular installments in *transition,* through 1938.

**1929**

*Ulysses* translated into French.

**1931**

Joyce and Nora marry in London July 4; Joyce's father dies in December.

**1932**

Joyce's grandson, Stephen James Joyce, born; Lucia Joyce has first mental breakdown.

**1933**

Judge John M. Woolsey of U.S. district court of New York rules *Ulysses* not pornographic.

**1934**

First American edition of *Ulysses* published by Random House; Frank Budgen publishes *James Joyce and the Making of* Ulysses.

**1936**

First British edition of *Ulysses.*

**1939**

Joyce publishes *Finnegans Wake;* World War II begins.

**1940**

Paris occupied by German military; Joyce and Nora flee Paris for Zurich.

**1941**

Joyce dies in Zurich January 13; buried at Fluntern Cemetery January 15; United States enters World War II.

# FOR FURTHER RESEARCH

## ABOUT JAMES JOYCE AND
## *A PORTRAIT OF THE ARTIST AS A YOUNG MAN*

Bernard Benstock, *Critical Essays on James Joyce.* Boston: G.K. Hall, 1985.

Sydney Bolt, *A Preface to James Joyce.* London: Longman, 1981.

David Daiches, *The Novel and the Modern World.* Chicago: University of Chicago Press, 1939.

A. Nicholas Fargnoli and Michael Patrick Gillespie, *James Joyce A to Z: The Essential Reference to the Life and Work.* New York: Oxford University Press, 1995.

Herbert Gorman, *James Joyce.* New York: Rinehart, 1939.

Kenneth Grose, *James Joyce.* Totowa, NJ: Rowman and Littlefield, 1975.

Stanislaus Joyce, *My Brother's Keeper: James Joyce's Early Years.* ed. Richard Ellmann. New York: Viking, 1958.

Frederick R. Karl, *The Contemporary English Novel.* New York: The Noonday Press, a subsidiary of Farrar, Straus and Giroux, 1962.

Hugh Kenner, *A Sinking Island: The Modern English Writers.* New York: Knopf, 1988.

Declan Kiberd, *Inventing Ireland.* Cambridge, MA: Harvard University Press, 1995.

James F. Kilroy, ed., *The Irish Short Story: A Critical History.* Boston: Twayne, 1984.

A. Walton Litz, *James Joyce.* New York: Twayne, 1966.

Arthur Power, *Conversations with James Joyce.* ed. Clive Hart. New York: Barnes & Noble, 1974.

J.I.M. Stewart, *Eight Modern Writers.* Oxford: Clarendon, 1963.

## ABOUT IRELAND AND EUROPE DURING JOYCE'S TIME

Bruce Bidwell and Linda Heffer, *The Joycean Way: A Topographic Guide to 'Dubliner' & 'A Portrait of the Artist as a Young Man.'* Dublin: Wolfhound Press, 1981.

E.H. Carr, *International Relations Between the Two World Wars, 1919–1939.* New York: St. Martin's, 1937.

Laurence Flanagan, Padraic O'Farrell, and Daithe O Hogain, *The Irish Spirit: Proverbs, Superstitions, and Fairy Tales.* New York: Gramercy Books, 1999.

Carlton J.H. Hayes and Margareta Faissler, *Modern Times: The French Revolution to the Present.* New York: Macmillan, 1966.

Patricia Hutchins, *James Joyce's World.* London: Methuen, 1957.

Thomas Keneally, *The Great Shame and the Triumph of the Irish in the English-Speaking World.* New York: Doubleday, 1998.

Seumas MacManus, *The Story of the Irish Race: A Popular History of Ireland.* Old Greenwich, CT: Wings Books, 1966.

Frank McCourt, *Angela's Ashes: A Memoir.* New York: Simon & Schuster, 1996.

David G. McCullough, ed., *The American Heritage Picture History of World War II.* New York: American Heritage, 1966.

John J.O. Reordain, *Irish Catholic Spirituality: Celtic and Roman.* Dublin: Columbia Press, 1996.

Cyril A. Reilly and Renee Travis Reilly, *An Irish Blessing: A Photographic Interpretation.* Notre Dame, IN: Sorin Books, 1999.

### NEWSLETTERS

*James Joyce Broadsheet.* For information, write to The Editors, *James Joyce Broadsheet,* The School of English, University of Leeds, Leeds LS29JT, England.

*James Joyce Newsletter.* For information, write to The Editors, *James Joyce Newsletter,* Department of English, Ohio State University, Columbus, OH 43210.

# INDEX